LOVING HARD-TO-LOVE PARENTS

*A Handbook for Adult Children
of Difficult Older Parents*

PAUL K. CHAFETZ, PHD

Copyright & Disclaimer

LOVING HARD-TO-LOVE PARENTS:
A HANDBOOK FOR ADULT CHILDREN
OF DIFFICULT OLDER PARENTS
Copyright © 2017 by Paul K. Chafetz PhD. All rights reserved.

Edited by Jon VanZile, Editing for Authors, Pompano Beach, FL
Layout by 52 Novels

Cover design by Pixelstudio, Bosnia and Herzegovina, through Fiverr.com

Original interior drawings by Maxtrella, Brazil, through Fiverr.com

Cover porcupine illustration from DepositPhotos.com

ISBN: 978-0-9990161-3-8

Printed in USA by Metro Graphics, Dallas, Texas

Please visit my website: PaulKChafetz.com

To my patients and their families,
with admiration, gratitude, and hope.

ENDORSEMENTS

"This book provides focused advice for dealing with difficult aging parents, a challenge that can cap off a lifetime of pain and distress within families. Written in manageable bites of information, Dr. Chafetz summarizes years of clinical experience into key principles that provide a framework for understanding and steps for action. Stories and illustrations keep it real. When no simplistic answers work, careful analysis of the options for balancing the needs of the family is critical. This books offers guidance for people in confusing situations."

> Sara Honn Qualls, PhD, ABPP
> Kraemer Family Professor of Aging Studies, Professor of Psychology
> Director, Aging Center and Gerontology Center
> Faculty Director, Lane Center for Academic Health Sciences
> University of Colorado–Colorado Springs

"Chock-filled with pearls of wisdom based on many years of laboring in the clinical trenches with this often-neglected population."

> Victor Molinari, PhD, ABPP
> Professor
> School of Aging Studies
> College of Behavioral and Community Sciences
> University of South Florida

"Dr. Chafetz's book is a must-read for anyone who has had to balance the responsibility of respecting their older parents with the painful necessity of having to 'put up with' unacceptable or destructive behaviors. When I was the primary caregiver for my mother who suffered with Alzheimer's, this book would have saved me from many sleepless nights! Full of practical tips that can be used *right now*, this book also alleviates the suffering that comes from:

- Feeling alone in the struggle and helpless to make a difference,
- Not understanding the origin of destructive behaviors, and
- The lack of effective boundaries."

Pam Boyd

Author of *Rescripting the workplace: Producing miracles with bosses, coworkers, and bad days* and other books.

www.dramaticconclusions.com

TABLE OF CONTENTS

FOREWORD

Child/parent relationships are changing dramatically in the twenty-first century. In fact, they are turning upside down. Increasingly, adult children are assuming a parental role for their aging and infirm parents. Although the goals of modern medicine and social policy are to keep us functional and comfortable from the beginning to the end of our lives, those lives are now longer—and with longevity there are greater periods of disability and dependency. The Social Security Administration estimates that persons sixty-five years of age can expect on average twenty additional years of life. Of those persons sixty-five or older, one in four may reach age ninety.

Most elders prefer to live independently and do not wish to be a financial, emotional, or physical burden for their children. However, the Administration on Aging reported in 2012 that nearly fifteen percent of elders were living below the poverty level. In addition, the American Association of Retired Persons reported in 2005 that nearly 70 percent of sixty-five-year olds were cognitively impaired or disabled in two or more activities of daily living.

It is clear, then, that adult children of elders will, in greater numbers and for greater periods of time, be entwined with their own parents.

Gero-psychologist Paul Chafetz offers aid and comfort to these adult children, especially those with strained or complicated relationships with one or more parent. His advice is not only for managing parents, but also preserving their children's quality of life. His style is gentle and conversational. His writing is clear. His suggestions are useful.

I commend this work by a wise and knowledgeable colleague.

Myron F. Weiner, MD
Professor Emeritus of Psychiatry
University of Texas Southwestern Medical Center
Dallas, Texas

GETTING STARTED

You probably know some truly fine people in their thirties to sixties whose older parents treat them really badly, with hurtful sarcasm, irrational demands, constant criticism, and undeserved anger. These frustrated, unappreciated adult sons and daughters simply want to be good to their parents. Perhaps you are one of these people yourself. I call these people "children of difficult older parents," or simply CODOP.

This book is about children of difficult older parents and the tools that I, with my clients' help, have developed over the past thirty years for helping them learn how to protect themselves emotionally, how to effectively love their hard-to-love older relatives, and how to create a healthy legacy for their own children. This book is a handbook for children of difficult older parents.

I believe the reason people face so many struggles and dilemmas in life, love, and loss is so they can learn from living and grow from learning. In short, life is for learning and growing!

Whether we are in our twenties, forties, sixties, or eighties, whatever adjustment life is asking us to make, we can grow into it! I believe this so firmly that I have adopted the phrase, "Grow into it with Dr. Paul," as my practice's motto. My job as a psychologist is to use my understanding of psychological concepts, insights, methods, and skills to help adults grow into their challenges and into their next stages.

The aim of this book is to provide tools to people everywhere who deal with difficult older parents, their own or others', so they may better grow into this challenging phase of life. This book is also for anyone who knows a child of a difficult older parent, who loves one, or who wants to be prepared to help one they might one day meet, including mental health professionals, members of the clergy, and senior care professionals.

My aha moment

I moved to Dallas, Texas, in 1982, after completing my doctoral studies in clinical psychology and finishing a two-year post-doctoral fellowship in clinical geriatric psychology. Every day for the next twenty years, my private practice took me into every corner of the local senior care network. Naturally, I met only the occasional difficult person, because the vast majority of people I encountered were fine, honorable, and well-meaning. I noticed, however, that the elderly individuals who were the focus of my psychological consultations were often described quite explicitly as very difficult.

This is how I identified the simple fact that not every older adult is delightful.

I began paying special attention to the struggles faced by the adult children of these difficult parents. Every week I heard some variation of, "My mom is driving me crazy!" or, "She is making me nuts!" or, "I don't know what to do!"

Listening to and learning from these adult children became my passion. I began collecting their strategies, both successful and not so successful. In working directly with these adult children, I witnessed many of them forging their own resolve to turn their emotional desperation into a constructive action plan. They found ways to turn this challenge into the building blocks of a better self. They often discovered that the silver lining of having a difficult relative was unexpected personal growth.

My exposure to so many cases fortuitously positioned me to compile their experiences and add my own innovations. For thirty-five years, I have found it personally rewarding to gradually refine these techniques and witness how helpful they proved to my subsequent clients. The result is this book.

Why another book about difficult parents?

A staggering number of books have been published with some variation on the title *Dealing With Difficult People*, including some specifically on the topic of difficult parents. Many are excellent and deserve your attention. Clearly, this is a widespread challenge in life.

Yet I believe this book is unique. It contains ten key concepts, ten key insights, and ten key behavioral skills I have formulated from my experience with hundreds of adult children of difficult older parents. It is your toolbox of essential, immediately applicable concepts, insights, and skills.

Is CODOP an ageist concept?

You might wonder if limiting this discussion to difficult *older* parents implies that I believe there is something about advanced age that makes parents—or anybody—difficult. Am I just negative about old people? Am I granny-bashing?

Absolutely not.

Today's older parents span three remarkable generations (more correctly called "cohorts"). The oldest is the GI generation, also called the Greatest Generation (born 1910–1925), who survived childhood in the Great Depression and went on to sacrifice their youth to save much of the world from fascism. The middle is the silent or traditional generation (born 1926–1945) who experienced economic hardship and then wartime restrictions in youth. They went on fight in WWII, Korea, and even Vietnam, but they also launched the Civil Rights movement. The youngest is the Boomer generation (born 1946–1964), who parlayed post-war prosperity into greater freedom and individuality, amazing artistic and commercial creativity, and extensive revision of outmoded social norms. The vast majority of individuals in all three cohorts are honorable, pleasant, and productive people.

My work with adult children of difficult older parents is not about age. It is about the pattern of unpleasant behavior shown by certain adults toward their own offspring. This package of tools for adult children of difficult older parents is an effort to minimize and heal the psychological damage caused by bad or disordered behavior.

PART ONE

The Difficult Older Parent & Their Adult Child

Adult children of difficult older parents can have a difficult father, a difficult mother, or less commonly, two difficult parents.

Typical descriptions of difficult fathers

"He has a horrible temper and is a chronic liar. My passive and fearful mom was completely beaten down by him."

"He has always been critical, negative, argumentative, overbearing, and verbally abusive. He alienates everybody."

"He was usually on the road as a salesman. When home, he drank too much, had a raging temper, and abused us verbally and physically. He was cruel."

"My dad was odd. He has always been detached, not close with anybody. He was critical of everything I did. He killed every dream I had."

"My father was cruel. He was cold, harsh, and critical. He was often unfaithful to my mom. She was a devoted wife, but weak and afraid of him."

"My dad is a very successful businessman and very narcissistic."

Typical descriptions of difficult mothers

"Mom has always been unpredictable. Her attitude toward you could be sweet, but could turn vicious in a heartbeat. She has always had a rage habit, and she could aim it at anybody."

"My mother was a hateful bitch. I know she had some painful losses as a girl, and may have been sexually abused, but that doesn't justify her being as cold, impossible, and controlling as she was to me. What's more, she was that way only to me. She treated my brothers like little princes, then and now. I was Dad's favorite. He was brilliant and stoic. At least he was safe for me."

"Mom could not stand for any of us kids to be friends with anyone but her. Anytime I mentioned to her that I had met a nice person, she found out who it was, gave them a call, told them some lies about me, and they wouldn't have anything to do with me again."

"Mom was a socialite, a real extrovert. You know, high society, inherited money. She was widely beloved for her charitable generosity and her magnificent parties. To me, though, she was never affectionate. In fact, she was rude to me. She called me stupid a lot, and violated my trust and confidences all the time. She had Dad trained to keep quiet. He didn't have much money or income."

"Mother has always been tough as nails. She is beautiful and wealthy, but unforgiving, unrelentingly demanding, rejecting, consuming, smothering, and angry. She never once told me she loved me. Dad married her for her beauty and learned fast to keep his head down."

"Mom is a first-generation American. Her immigrant mom was really hard on her. To my sister and me, Mom was impossible. Incredibly selfish and mean, she abused us mentally and physically. She was secretive but expected us to read her mind. We often got the silent treatment, knowing she was unhappy with us but not knowing why or how to fix it. There were frequent spankings. She teased us and would humiliate us in front of others. She had no friends, but ruled our home totally. Dad was a gentle, passive pleaser who was just crushed by Mom."

"Mom told me, 'You know that your sister really hates you, don't you?' I later learned that she told my sister the same thing about me."

"My mom liked nobody! She criticized us all continually, but tried hard to keep me and my sister from leaving home. She didn't support my going off to college, and she used lies and deceit to ruin my sister's marriage. She was a malicious gossiper and was often unfaithful to Dad."

"Mom always drank a lot. She was demanding to the point of being impossible to please. She has always been totally spoiled and self-centered, and nothing has ever been her fault. She always just criticized and blamed everyone else, especially me. She manipulated Dad throughout their marriage."

"My mother is callous, careless, caustic, cold, complaining, condemning, critical, cruel, and cutting. That's just the C words. I could go on."

Typical descriptions of difficult mother/father pairs

"Mom was Dad's first wife. She was usually warm and loving, but often criticized me and my sister unfairly. Dad was terrible. He was always angry. He was domineering, closed off, and distant. He'd hit me if my grades weren't good enough. He only stopped because I got too big to hit. He and Mom divorced, and he's had two more divorces since then."

"I grew up with my parents fighting all the time. They married young, and both were a mess to begin with. Dad grew up poor and lost his mom early. He was never supportive of me, only critical. Mom was cold and distant, never affectionate. She never taught me anything. Neither of them ever had any idea how to love another person."

"My parents both grew up in huge and kind of crazy families. Dad had terrible self-esteem and feared failure and shame. He was very secretive and had severe social anxiety. He taught us all to avoid getting to know people or letting them know us. Mom was unhappy with him, but too passive to do anything about it. Sometimes she would get drunk, and then her resentment would come out big time. I am thankful that I found a wonderful wife who helped me escape that home situation."

"My dad had a fancy education, but never made a great living. Still, he has been pushy, difficult, demanding, and disrespectful to us forever. Mom has always hated his behavior, but her ways of coping with him were pretty terrible, too. Instead of speaking up for herself, she is a professional victim. It's always, 'Poor me!' She walks around pouting, making faces, and hinting at her complaints. It was so painful when I was small. Now it's just disgusting."

What about you?

The parental behaviors listed below are common in the descriptions I hear in my practice from adult children of difficult older parents. How many apply to your experience of your parents?

Your older parent currently...

1. Abuses alcohol, illicit drugs, or prescription medications.
2. Is unfairly critical of you, or impossible to please.
3. Makes irrational demands on you.
4. Frequently complains to you about everything.
5. Phones you too often or at inappropriate times of day.
6. Blames you for their difficulties or unhappiness in life.
7. Is ungrateful for, or uncooperative with, your efforts to be helpful (e.g., fires caregivers).
8. Shows you undeserved anger or rudeness.
9. Is dismissive, sarcastic, or otherwise hurtful toward you or those close to you.
10. Ignores or denies news or instructions from doctors or other professionals that they should change certain behaviors (such as diet, driving, hygiene, medications, money management, or living arrangements), resulting in neglect of their own health, safety, or well-being.
11. Denies their declining ability to care for themselves.
12. Is a hoarder.
13. Is giving and delightful with friends, but surly and unpleasant with you, showing more regard for "appearances" and other people than for you and your feelings.
14. Gossips maliciously or seems to like nobody.
15. Disparages you to others.
16. Betrays your confidences.
17. Is vain and spoiled, or otherwise self-centered and selfish.
18. Has become highly repetitive.
19. Has begun showing terrible judgment with people, such as agreeing to be friends or lovers with new, shady characters.

20. Has begun showing terrible judgment with money, such as giving or "loaning" money to strangers or buying foolishly online, by phone, or by mail.

21. Has become an unsafe driver, yet refuses to stop driving.

22. Has become an unsafe cook, yet refuses to stop cooking.

23. Has become more irritable, even aggressive toward you or others, and is unaware that their behavior is inappropriate.

24. Has begun to neglect their hygiene or appearance and is unconcerned about this, thus endangering their health and their social connections.

When you were young, your parent...

1. Abused alcohol or drugs.

2. Gave you the silent treatment, or otherwise withheld love and connection.

3. Threatened to send you away or leave you.

4. Taught you that the world was a cold, unfair, or dangerous place that would not welcome you.

5. Criticized you excessively, or was impossible to please. Belittled you or teased you in public or in private. Told you that you were not good enough or would never succeed.

6. Gossiped maliciously or seemed to like nobody.

7. Prevented you from making or keeping friends. Ran off potential or actual friends or mates. Discouraged you from leaving home (e.g., going to college, getting married).

8. Imposed their preferences on all of your choices, activities, and behaviors (demanding, controlling).

9. Hit you, bullied you, or cursed at you.

10. Touched you in sexual ways, or almost never touched you.

11. Frequently lied to you, or let you witness them lying to others. Encouraged you to lie or keep many secrets.

12. Was giving and delightful around friends, but surly and unpleasant around you, showing more regard for "appearances" and other people than for you.

13. Openly criticized your other parent, pushing you to take sides.

14. Was vain and spoiled, or otherwise self-centered and selfish.

15. Failed to protect you from real or potential dangers. Did not anticipate or prevent dangerous situations for you. Neglected your pleasure, comfort, development, and well-being.
16. Was sexually promiscuous (e.g., unfaithful, provocative, immodest, involved with prostitutes). Brought many lovers into your home. Had sex with your boyfriend or girlfriend.
17. Was irresponsible with money (shopaholic, spendthrift), spending money needed for support and care of the family.
18. Was frankly crazy (hallucinatory, delusional).

When you were young, you often felt...

1. Afraid.
2. Unloved.
3. Confused.
4. More loved by a grandparent, aunt, uncle, or neighbor than by one parent or both.

Types of difficult-parent situations

There are many behavior patterns that create difficult-parent situations, and we can use these patterns to sort the variety of difficult-parent situations. I have found that the blood relationship between the adult child and the older individual actually makes little difference. Your difficult parent might be your biological parent, your step-parent, or your parent-in-law. He might even be an uncle, or he may not be biologically or legally related to you at all but has nevertheless played an intimate, parent-like role in your life.

In my experience, the vast majority of difficult-parent situations fall into a relatively short list of scenarios, each marked by a core difficult behavior. They may exhibit characteristics from more than one scenario. I have shaped this list into two parts.

By far, most difficult-parent situations I see involve parents who have been difficult for decades due to chronic personality issues. We will examine in depth the vital topic of personality disorders in Concept 6 on page 27. Reflecting the importance of this significant population, the first part of my list addresses what I call the classic six scenarios:

- **INTRUSIVENESS** refers to the parent who arrives at your home or office uninvited and then stays too long, ignoring normal social indicators that their visit is ill-timed. They may phone you too often or routinely try to pry into your private topics during conversation. They show up at your kids' sports events and push their way into your conversations with your friends.
- **LAZINESS** refers to the parent who is needy yet uncooperative. In many instances, they warrant the label of a "help-rejecting complainer." They neglect the management of themselves and their home. When you generously try to help in these tasks, the parent is unappreciative and passively obstructionist. Your help is blocked or undone, and the complaining continues.

- **BLAMING, CRITICISM** refers to the parent who is unapprecia-tive, crassly disrespectful, and hateful. This parent has a history of actively disparaging your character to your face and to others. As far as this parent is concerned, you never do anything right. Your accomplishments and assistance are dismissed or taken for granted, and all you hear from the parent is criticism.

- **DISHONESTY** refers to the parent who lies to you and others, betrays your confidence, reveals your secrets, and gossips about you and others. This parent never lets the truth stand in the way of a good story. This parent does not hesitate to bend or break the truth to serve their convenience, win them social points, or protect their pride.

- **IRRESPONSIBILITY** refers to the parent who recklessly squan-ders their own or their child's resources or endangers themselves or others, and accepts no accountability for their actions. This parent has poor judgment, foolishly trusts the untrustworthy stranger, and expends no effort to protect themselves from exploitation or dan-ger. They spend excessively, impulsively, and selfishly, keep company with questionable individuals, or otherwise neglect their own safety. Either through addiction to sweepstakes or lotteries or having na-ively fallen into a web of con men and scams, they are systematically separated from their money. They may go to dangerous locations, dress in ways that draw inappropriate attention, or provoke con-flict with strangers. Yet they refuse to accept guidance from their children.

- **INNOCENT FAÇADE** refers to the parent who treats everyone else better than they do you. Few or none of their friends have ever seen the parent behave meanly to you, and therefore would find it difficult to believe your description of your parent's difficult behav-ior. This parent presents a misleadingly pleasant face to the public and creates a private hell for the child. The parent's hypocritical, two-faced behavior leaves the adult child constantly wondering which persona is their parent's authentic one. The child's normal, lifelong instinct and desire to trust the parent is chronically and perversely blocked by the outwardly normal parent's cruelly disap-proving treatment.

In contrast to these classic six scenarios involving long-difficult parents, the second part of my list is what I call the cognitive six scenarios, which are found in parents who have become newly difficult with the onset of dementia:

- **REPETITIVENESS** refers to the parent who says the same thing dozens of times a day. It may be asking the same question or voicing the same complaint. The cognitively impaired parent does not remember saying it before, and certainly does not remember the response the adult child gave. You quickly realize that responding logically every time is pointless, but you see no alternative.
- **RESTLESSESS** refers to the parent who shows frequent anxiety, worry, or fear. This behavior often seems more severe in the afternoon, which is why it is often called sundowning.
- **WANDERING** refers to the parent who walks to the wrong places, at the wrong times, or just too much. Trespassing is going into other people's spaces. Eloping is leaving the premises in a way that is somehow inappropriate, such as underdressed, unsafe, or too confused to be able to return home on their own. Pacing is incessant or excessive walking. In most cases, it is very difficult to know how consciously purposeful the walking is.
- **DELUSION** refers to the parent who has an inaccurate belief and lets no evidence or facts change the belief. If the delusion involves the idea that someone has evil intent toward the parent (e.g., theft, assault, dislike), it is called paranoid. It might also be jealous, romantic, or grandiose. One very strange delusion, caused by a certain form of brain disease, is Capgras, in which the patient believes that someone, usually a spouse, is not really the spouse, but rather an identical-appearing imposter.
- **AGGRESSION, ANGER, IRRITIBILITY** refers to the parent whose words, tone, or actions show hostility.
- **DEPRESSION, WITHDRAWAL, LETHARGY** refers to the parent who has little or no energy to move around, participate in any activities, or interact with people. They appear to care about nothing or to have given up on life.

These twelve scenarios probably include the situation you face. In PART THREE: IMPLEMENTATION, I will identify the concepts, insights, and skills that are most essential in addressing each difficult-parent situation. But all thirty tools that follow are relevant to all of these difficult-parent situations. So I advise you, just as the wagon train pioneers to the American West were cautioned, "Take no shortcuts and hurry along as fast as you can."

The biggest issues and needs of adult children of difficult older parents

In February 2016, I convened a focus group of a dozen adult children of difficult older parents in Dallas. The participants were volunteers who responded to solicitations I distributed among my network of senior-living industry professionals. Of course, I had already worked with hundreds of such family members throughout my thirty-plus years of psychology practice. Yet the focus group was my first opportunity to meet such adult children who had not sought out psychotherapy with me and to ask them one basic question: "What are your biggest issues and needs related to having a difficult older parent?" I learned a lot from the focus group.

I discovered that three issues typify life for adult children of difficult older parents: exhaustion, demoralization, and disappointment. Here is why:

- They find it exhausting to contend with many unpleasant emotions, including anger, embarrassment, fear, frustration, guilt, helplessness, loneliness, resentment, and sadness.
- They are demoralized from their long history of seeing typical interaction styles and methods (such as reasoning) repeatedly fail to keep the peace with their difficult parent, even though they reliably promote peaceful relationships with other people.
- They are deeply disappointed due to the many frustrating or unsatisfying experiences with the mental health professionals they have consulted about their difficult parents. They are left feeling betrayed and alone.

I also learned they are hungry for help with four needs:

- Support from people who really understand their dilemma.
- Effective tools for understanding their parent.

- Skills for responding constructively to their parent.
- Safeguards against becoming a difficult parent to their own children.

I am grateful to the focus group members for sharing their stories so openly with me and with each other. Their input reinforced and deepened my understanding of their struggle. Their contributions are helping shape my work with adult children of difficult older parents in Dallas and beyond.

The CODOP program

My program for these adults has three goals. They are that children of difficult older parents learn how to:

1. protect their heart,
2. effectively love their hard-to-love older relatives, and
3. create a healthy legacy for their children.

The program presented in this book offers a new toolbox for achieving these goals and transitioning or growing into a more mature state. The toolbox includes three sets of growth strategies. The strategies begin with ten concepts to empower your mind. These are principles that form the foundation for the remaining twenty tools. Second are ten insights to comfort your heart. These are ideas and understandings that pertain to the emotional, ethical, and philosophical aspects of your challenges. The third are ten skills to guide your actions. These are concrete steps to implement through your own behavior.

The ten concepts and the ten insights alone can dramatically ease your intellectual confusion and emotional pain, and this welcome internal change may even be visible to others. However, it is through applying the ten skills that the world will recognize that you are mastering your dilemma. Not every skill will fit your situation, but all of them will be tools you can use as the need arises.

My promise to you is that, after reading this book, you will know the ten concepts, realize the ten insights, and be ready to practice the ten skills.

Are you ready? Let's begin!

PART TWO

New Tools for Building a Better Future

It is often said that humans are distinguished from other species by our use of tools. From the first club to the electron microscope and interplanetary satellites, our advancement has been a steady march toward increasingly sophisticated tools. Every project a person undertakes requires tools, and the right tools make success both easier and more likely. The amazing thing about many tools is that, after being used to accomplish the task at hand, they can be cleaned and stored, ready to be redeployed when needed.

Here are the thirty most powerful tools for adult child of difficult older parents I have identified in my thirty-five years of practice. They are grouped into three categories: ten concepts to empower your mind, ten insights to comfort your heart, and ten skills to guide your actions.

Ten Concepts to Empower Your Mind

"Never underestimate the value of an idea."
—CHINONYE J. CHIDOLUE

I begin with the most abstract and fundamental tools: concepts. The concepts and insights that precede the skills are fundamental to my worldview as a psychologist. You will find them to have wide application in life, and some may even seem profound. You will find yourself pausing to consider the many ways each is operating in your life, and learning how to forge them into a customized solution for your challenges.

Concept 1. Lifespan development occurs in stages

"If we were all pears, our parents might tell us, it is perfectly normal to be green before you are golden."
—TOM ALTHOUSE, THE FROWNY FACE COW

Humans grow. Therefore change (also called development) is absolutely inevitable. This change is considered not only normal or typical, but healthy and desirable. The time frame of a human's development is lifelong. Humans develop in predictable steps tied loosely to a schedule, so no one should ever be surprised when they reach their next step.

In short, life can be a journey of exciting discovery and continual learning, which moves through a series of normal, healthy, and predictable life challenges. Josh Prager puts it well in his book, *100 Years: Wisdom*

From Famous Writers on Every Year of Your Life (2016): "Here were the wonders and confinements of childhood, the emancipations and frustrations of adolescence, the empowerments and millstones of adulthood, and the recognitions and resignations of old age. There were patterns to life, and they were shared."

There is always something to anticipate—because under the right circumstances we grow and learn our way through life! Most of us gradually leave naiveté and immaturity behind. We do this growing, maturing, and learning in *stages*. There have been many popular examples of life stages. Probably the best known are Shakespeare's seven ages of man, Freud's five stages, and, of particular relevance here, Eric Erikson's eight stages.

The noted psychoanalyst Erikson organized the human lifespan into eight developmental stages extending from birth to death. Since adulthood covers a span of many years, Erikson divided adulthood into the experiences of young adults, middle-aged adults, and older adults. For each stage, he identified a psychosocial struggle between a desirable outcome and an undesirable outcome.

In young adulthood, roughly between ages eighteen and thirty-five, the possible outcomes are either intimacy and solidarity or isolation. Following closely on the completion of adolescence, when independence is established, the outcome in young adulthood depends on how well the individual acquires the basic strengths of affiliation and love.

In middle adulthood, roughly ages thirty-five to fifty-five or sixty-five, we tend toward either generativity or self-absorption and stagnation. In this stage, when our resources and social power are usually at their peak, we are called upon to apply these to the betterment of others. We take responsibility, and we sacrifice our convenience, for the well-being and progress of our families, our communities, and our world. We develop the basic strengths of production and care.

In late adulthood, covering ages fifty-five or sixty-five to death, Erikson identified the ego development outcome as either integrity or despair. At this stage, individuals look back on their life and see both happy and unhappy times, commendable and uncommendable actions, desirable and regrettable outcomes. They then conclude either that it is

OK that the past was as it was, leading to pride and contentment, or that it is not OK. In this case, they either blame themselves and get depressed, or they blame others and show chronic anger and bitter resentment. The desired basic strength is wisdom.

In 1998, Erikson's ninety-three-year-old wife, Joan Erikson, recommended adding another stage to the model to correspond to a period of final functional decline, usually in one's eighties and nineties.

Erikson's framework has since been joined by other theories and stage models of adult development, and its value is probably more theoretical than scientific. It remains, however, a very useful and widely respected tool that offers many insights.

The percentage of people who successfully complete each transition in life is extremely high. People succeed by growing into their next stage.

Concept 2. Stages are bridged by transitions

"Everybody has talent, but ability takes hard work."
—MICHAEL JORDAN

As mentioned above, life is a journey of continual growth, and we develop through a succession of stages. Our stages are not limited to the decades-long stages described by Erikson; stages are also smaller, such as entering fifth grade, going on one's first date, or deciding to marry. Every "first" heralds a new stage and often involves getting or losing something, such as a job, a relationship, or an important possession.

Stages are bridged by transitions, and every transition presents us with the opportunity to learn and grow. As a result, life is a nearly continuous series of myriad stages, and we are virtually always in transition from one stage into another.

Every psychological transition has three components: emotional, intellectual, and behavioral. More specifically, each person's three-part recipe for growing into their future should be to (a) understand, process, and master the emotions stirred up by the transition, (b) learn the new skills we will need for the next stage, and (c) put real effort, hard work, into moving forward successfully. This is our job.

In fact, people poised at the start of a new life stage have already outgrown their previous stage. Just as a fetus will die if it does not strive and struggle to emerge from its mother, or a chick will die if it does not work at breaking out of the shell, so anyone poised at the start of a new stage of life must address the three components of their transition.

Although not always comfortable or easy, it is nevertheless good and healthy to be in transition. It means we are moving forward, not stagnating. Most of us grow wiser with the passing years. It seems, though, that to learn everything a person should know, we would have to live about seven hundred years! Most of us only get about a tenth of this time, so none of us has any time to waste.

Concept 3. Normal aging

"Aging is not lost youth but a new stage of opportunity and strength."
—BETTY FRIEDAN

There is widespread misunderstanding of what normal psychological aging looks like. The common perception is a very negative picture. Therefore, many people attribute any unpleasant behavior in older adults to advanced age. This is usually unjustified. In reality, most older adults are content, capable, and connected.

Let's look first at the emotional life of typical older adults. A 2016 study by Michael Thomas and colleagues of 1,546 randomly selected adults between twenty-one and one hundred years of age confirmed the results of many previous studies that, despite significant declines in physical health and cognitive function, the mental health of adults improves with advancing age. Gero-psychologists call this the "paradox of well-being."

Researchers have shown that additional years of life produce more effective skill at regulating one's emotions. Not only are groups of older adults better at actively and purposefully maintaining, transforming, and discontinuing social relationships, they also consistently report fewer negative emotional experiences and greater emotional stability than do groups of younger adults.

The belief, prevalent in the 1970s, that depression was the "common cold" of later life is now known to be not only incorrect, but upside down. The prevalence of major depressive disorder in adults consistently falls with age. In fact, the only mental disorder that becomes more common with advanced age is dementia. All others either decrease or are unchanged with age. I think these findings are quite heartening. We can all look forward to lower risks of depression as we move into our future.

Next, what about older adults' desire for social connection? If you had to guess, which group of adults, aged twenty-five, forty-five, or sixty-five, are most interested in making new friends? Psychologist Laura Carstensen of Stanford University has been studying life-span changes in emotional experience, regulation, and control for the past twenty-five years. She co-created Socio-Emotional Selectivity Theory (Carstensen, et al., 1999), which not only answers the above question but provides a surprising explanation for the answer. The theory proposes and the data demonstrate, not surprisingly, that in general adolescents and young adults are more interested in exploration, novelty, new knowledge, and new relationships than are older adults. Conversely, older adults, on average, are more interested in routine, emotional comfort, familiarity, and deepening existing relationships.

The reason, however, is not their age. Rather, the reason is how much longer the individual expects to be alive, which the researchers call "perceived time." The shorter one's perceived time, the more strongly most adults at any age prefer familiar relationships over new relationships. This includes, for example, young adults who are seriously ill or engaged in a violent lifestyle likely to bring their early demise. Typically, younger adults expect many more decades, so they are eager to spread out their emotional energy. They assume they can deepen and savor their "old" links many years later, due to their greater perceived time.

What about the thinking ability of older adults? The definitive study of how the strength of various forms of thinking ability fares across the adult lifespan comes from the University of Washington in Seattle. Since testing the first large sample of adults in 1963, the Seattle Longitudinal Study has tracked and retested a series of representative samples of adults about every seven years throughout the adult years regarding their cognitive abilities. They have demonstrated that the various mental abilities improve into the late fifties, then level off, then, in the absence of a dementing disease, gradually decline a small amount into the later years. In short, most older adults have mental sharpness that is perfectly adequate for daily living. Dementia is not typical aging.

Concept 4. Where does personality come from?

"Everyone has a story. Every story matters."
—NICOLE WEDEMEYER MILLER

Healthy personalities, that is, individuals' consistent patterns of feeling, thinking, and behaving, come in many flavors. It is important to note that very diverse personalities can all be considered healthy and normal. Normal is a very wide range, indeed. Still, I am often asked, "Dr. Paul, why is my parent like that? Why are people the way they are? What made them into the type of person they are?" My answer is always that a person's personality is formed by influences from three sources: nature, nurture, and choices.

Nature refers to the fact that each person is born into this world with a certain set of character predispositions. Some people are intrinsically more hardy and resilient than others and less distressed by tribulations, conflict, or stress. Some are more naturally attuned than others to the behaviors and feelings of people around them.

Nurture refers to all the experiences that living in the world creates. We experience a certain family life, which is perhaps warm and accepting or perhaps harshly punitive or dangerously neglectful. We experience a certain economic and societal environment, perhaps characterized by wealth with many educational opportunities or perhaps by war, economic deprivation, or ethnic discrimination. We may be treated as attractive and welcomed, or we may be hated and rejected.

Finally, whatever one's nature and nurture have been, each of us makes our own decisions or choices about what kind of a person we wish to be. Most commonly, positive influences from nature and nurture make it easier to grow into a psychologically healthy individual who behaves responsibly and constructively, seeing and treating themselves and others kindly and fairly. We see a minority of people, however, who, despite having had every advantage in their background, somehow turn into unhappy and unpleasant individuals. Likewise, there are many inspiring stories of individuals who grew up with many strikes against them and seemingly every justification for becoming bitter and selfish, yet nevertheless *choose* to live a life of cooperation, generosity, selflessness, productivity, and optimism.

It is this key role of personal choice that creates hope that anyone can turn their life in a more positive direction. Through effort applied in effective psychotherapy and practice in real life, most people can overcome toxic influences and heal old wounds. Quite often, these people emerge more resilient, mature, and interesting than people who had no old wounds to repair and no toxic influences to overcome! Few things in life give me more satisfaction than being part of my patients' journey toward this state of being. Remember, we grow and learn our way through life.

Concept 5. Coping mechanisms

"If you aren't in over your head, how do you know how tall you are?"
—T.S. ELIOT

"Every one of us is a minor tragedy. Most of us learn to cope."
—ELIZABETH BEAR, WHISKEY AND WATER

People make the oddest choices!

Another question I often hear from adults about their difficult older parent is, "What is my mother *thinking* when she acts this way?! How can she really believe she is doing the right thing?" My opinion, after thirty-five years of practicing psychology, is that everybody is doing the best they know how to do with their situation.

Every person has an unconscious mind, and everyone's unconscious is devoted 100 percent to emotional survival. The key component of emotional survival is freedom from emotional pain in general and, most particularly, maintaining an adequately positive self-image, free from shame, guilt, or humiliation.

The unconscious pursues its goal of emotional comfort by using defense mechanisms. These are the various ways that our minds automatically modify our experience of reality to avoid emotional discomfort and keep us from acting on unacceptable impulses. To the surprise of many, we now know that the number of defense mechanisms reaches nearly fifty! Psychoanalyst George Vaillant (2011) divided our defense mechanisms into four categories. From worst to best, his categories are called psychotic (e.g., delusional projection), immature (e.g., dissociation or projection), neurotic (e.g., acting out, displacement, isolation, or repression), and mature (e.g., altruism, sublimation, suppression, and humor).

In my clinical experience,[1] I have found that almost every person with a difficult personality is uncomfortable inside. They have a painful dilemma in living, which their conscious mind may only dimly recognize. However, their unconscious feels it acutely and is actively striving to manage it. Their unconscious, therefore, makes strategic adjustments in their perception of the world, of themselves, and of you, all for the purpose of easing their inner discomfort. These distorted perceptions dictate and justify their behaviors, which can result in the unpleasant behaviors other people witness. This strategy is somewhat successful, so they continue using it. Tragically, the distress they cause you temporarily reduces their inner pain—but this is the best solution they have found so far for limiting their psychic pain.

Note that it is precisely this inner pain that drives their difficult behavior. In other words, their unpleasant behavior toward you is all about them and their search for relief from inner pain. It is really not about you at all! Their verbal claim that their distress is about you reflects the distortion of reality that is occurring inside their psyche.

This distortion, which is shaped and triggered by emotions, is not amenable to logical rebuttal. True, the difficult person's complaints about you are spoken in coherent language with proper grammar and adult vocabulary, and therefore they have the trappings of rationality. In reality, though, they are the product of unconscious defense mechanisms that do not obey the rules of logic. That is why efforts to use logic, facts, and

---

1. My clinical experience has not included individuals who commit truly terrible deeds like murder, kidnapping, rape, mutilation, etc. I may not propose such a benevolent theory to explain their behavior.

reasoning to change their opinions, improve their mood, or normalize their behavior will never be very successful. Your experience of repeatedly trying yet failing to reason them out of their irrational complaints about you proves this point.

Concept 6. Personality disorders

Mental health professionals recognize many broad types of mental disorders. Everyone is familiar with mood disorders such as major depression or bipolar disorder, thought disorders such as schizophrenia, and neurocognitive disorders such as dementia. However, many people are not aware of the important type of disorder called disorders of adult personality and behavior. The *International Classification of Diseases, 10th Edition (ICD-10)* defines personality disorders (PDs) generally as follows:

- A diverse category of psychiatric disorders characterized by behavior that deviates markedly from the expectations of the individual's culture; this pattern of deviation is pervasive and inflexible and is stable over time. The behavioral pattern negatively interferes with relationships and work.
- A major deviation from normal patterns of behavior.
- Personality disorders are long-term patterns of thoughts and behaviors that cause serious problems with relationships and work. People with personality disorders have difficulty dealing with everyday stresses and problems. They often have stormy relationships with other people. Symptoms vary widely depending on the specific type of personality disorder.
- When normal personality traits become inflexible and maladaptive, causing subjective distress or impaired social functioning, they can be considered disorders.

The ICD-10 lists nine specific personality disorders (paranoid, schizoid, antisocial, borderline, histrionic, obsessive-compulsive, avoidant, dependent, and narcissistic) and allows for an "unspecified" personality disorder that does not fit cleanly into the specific criteria.

There is a very important point here. In personality disorders, the individual looks and acts in most ways just like anyone else. They neither look "crazy" nor complain of being unhappy. Yet decades of research and the experience and opinion of hundreds of thousands of mental health professionals substantiate the fact that personality disorders are real and can be very severe. I believe that when the child of a difficult older parent realizes that this "pathology masquerading as normalcy" is not normal, the child can begin escaping the emotional force field created by the difficult individual's behavior. In short, learning about personality disorders is a vital tool in the child's pursuit of emancipation and empowerment.

Studies of adults in the US find that the prevalence of at least one PD is between 9 percent and 15 percent. The most common are obsessive-compulsive and paranoid PDs. Unfortunately, scientists do not yet have good data about the prevalence of personality disorders in older adults. In fact, several of the PDs have diagnostic criteria that are often not even relevant to older adults, such as impaired work performance. However, there are strong indications that, in general and on average, advancing age reduces the severity and prevalence of antisocial PD, borderline PD, histrionic PD, and narcissistic PD, as well as dependent PD and avoidant PD. In contrast, obsessive-compulsive PD and schizoid PD may somewhat rise in prevalence. These average effects of age, of course, cannot predict the behavior of any one individual.

The specific personality disorders listed in the ICD-10 form the building blocks of the knowledge for the child of a difficult older parent. Let's look a little more closely at the PDs that appear most often in difficult older parents, and their specific characteristics.

First, narcissistic PD is likely to include:

- An exaggerated sense of one's own abilities and achievements.
- A constant need for attention, affirmation, and praise.
- A belief that he or she is unique or "special" and should only associate with other people of the same status.
- Persistent fantasies about attaining success and power.
- Exploiting other people for personal gain.
- A sense of entitlement and expectation of special treatment (Expects much from others, and expects to have little demanded of themselves).
- A preoccupation with power or success.

- Feeling envious of others, or believing that others are envious of him or her.
- A lack of empathy for others.

Second, borderline PD is likely to include:

- Intense anger and aggressive behavior.
- Abandonment sensitivity.
- Unstable and intense interpersonal relationships.
- Unstable self-image, self-concept, or sense of self.
- Risky or impulsive behaviors.
- Emotional ups and downs.
- Self-harm behaviors.
- Suicide gestures or attempts.

Third, histrionic PD is likely to include:

- Displays of excessive but shallow emotions and attention-seeking behaviors.
- Rapid shifts of moods, opinions, and beliefs.
- Excessive need for others to witness their emotional displays.
- Exaggerated symptoms of weakness or illness.

Fourth, dependent PD is likely to include:

- A chronic and pervasive pattern of dependent, submissive, and needy behavior.
- Excessive seeking of advice, approval, and encouragement.
- Sensitivity to criticism or rejection.
- Low self-confidence and self-esteem.
- Inability to make decisions without direction from others.
- Feelings of helplessness when alone.
- Inability to disagree with others.
- Extreme devastation when close relationships end and a need to immediately begin a new relationship.

Of equal value to the several specific PDs is the existence of the "unspecified" form of PD. I have found that difficult older adults very often do not meet the official criteria of any single PD, but do show symptoms from two or three PDs, and therefore are best labeled "PD, unspecified."

I am often asked, "Are difficult older parents numerous or rare?" My belief, based on the population prevalence figures generated by research and on my practice experience, is that the prevalence in the general population is in the range of 5 percent to 10 percent. Labeling this number rare or too frequent is a matter of opinion.

Concept 7. Dementia

> "My husband is leaving me. No dramas, no slammed doors—well,
> OK, a few slammed doors—and no suitcase in the hall, but
> there is another woman involved. Her name is Dementia."
> —LAURIE GRAHAM

The human brain has a structure that is very well known, and, due to scientific advances, better understood every day. Different brain regions are responsible for different types of thinking. For example, word finding, memory, orientation in space, and judgment are all primarily handled by different brain regions. The accurate term for a significant and permanent reduction in the adult brain's ability to think is dementia. The type of thinking impairment differs depending on the cause of the dementia and the specific brain areas affected. This is why Alzheimer's disease produces symptoms and a course of disease that are different from those of dementia caused by a major stroke or a severe blow to the head.

There is a widespread misconception that all or most older adults get Alzheimer's disease or some other dementing disorder. In fact, only 5–8 percent of adults age 65+ have dementia; among those age 80+, it is only 20 percent. Only at age ninety does prevalence reach 50 percent. Again, most older adults never become demented!

Of those unlucky older adults who do develop dementia, the most common cause is Alzheimer's disease (about 55 percent of cases). The second leading cause is stroke (about 20 percent of cases). The remainder is caused by relatively rare diseases, including Pick's disease, Parkinson's, head trauma, and chronic alcohol abuse.

Alzheimer's disease causes a gradually progressive dementing syndrome, in which the earliest symptoms include impairment of memory for new information, depressed or irritable mood, and withdrawal from challenging activities. It progresses through somewhat predictable and increasing levels of impairment for ten to twelve years, with increasing need for supervision and direct care. The final stage is total disability in thinking and self-care.

Current medications for Alzheimer's disease, such as Aricept and Namenda, have demonstrable ability to slow the decline of thinking ability. It is important to note, however, that these medicines do not stop or reverse the impairment process.

Any cognitive impairment should trigger a thorough medical and psychological evaluation. In many cases, treatable and reversible problems are detected, and dementia is avoided. When dementia is diagnosed, psychological care includes supportive counseling for the patient, caregiving skill-coaching for relatives and other caregivers, and grief support.

Concept 8. Values: Guiding principles for caregiving

"A ship that sails without a compass will get lost at sea."
—MATSHONA DHLIWAYO

"Boundaries are easier to manage when your values are well-defined."
—JOE JORDAN, SHARPEN YOUR LIFE: 52 STRATEGIC
MOMENTS TO CREATE A LIFETIME OF SUCCESS

Difficult people can turn up in any sphere of our lives. Luckily, we can fire a friend turned nemesis or distance ourselves from a difficult coworker. However, when the difficult person in question is not an acquaintance or coworker, but your own parent, the challenge is more serious. If you are an adult with a difficult older parent, firing your parent is hard. You feel a certain obligation to look after them and to maintain not just contact with them, but also a safety net under them.

How can an adult son or daughter of, for example, a narcissistic mother, an abusive father, a cruel mother, or an alcoholic father be caring to this parent without risking further emotional damage to themselves?

The key lies in selecting appropriate guiding principles for interacting with the difficult parent.

Under normal circumstances, when dealing with any adult we encounter in life, we fully respect their autonomy. We owe them honesty and full disclosure, because they generally accept responsibility for their own decisions and will bear on their own shoulders the consequences of their actions. This is true even if we disagree with the wisdom of their choices.

If, however, we view the adult's unpleasant behavior as due to a personality disorder or a dementing brain disease, and we therefore see them as impaired rather than intentionally difficult, then our guiding principles for relating to them must change. Since most difficult parents' ability to accept responsibility for their own actions is impaired by either a personality disorder or a brain disorder, the adult child of difficult older parents should consider giving less priority to the parent's autonomy than healthy people deserve.

In place of autonomy, our guiding principles in relating to the impaired parent should be a commitment to their safety and dignity. This shift has important action implications. Most importantly, it directs the child of a difficult older parent to prioritize meeting the parent's *needs* over meeting the parent's *wants*. As any healthy adult recognizes, having one's needs met is mandatory; having one's wants met is optional, a luxury. Loving hard-to-love parents entails less obeying their wishes and more protecting them from themselves.

This concept is indispensable as the child of a difficult older parent becomes empowered to maturely tolerate their difficult parent's unavoidable distress and promote their parent's well-being despite the parent's resistance.

Concept 9. Authority and responsibility

"With great power there must also come great responsibility!"
—SPIDERMAN'S (PETER PARKER'S) UNCLE BEN

I believe that, to achieve family happiness, all adults must understand this: the people who take the most responsibility in a given area must be granted the most authority in that area. I repeat, the people who take the most responsibility in a given area must be granted the most authority in that area. As the saying goes, "At home, the cook decides how to spice the soup."

Responsibility refers to doing the work, putting in one's own money, time, or effort, and generally "carrying the load" for a certain project, such as caring for oneself or an impaired relative. Authority is the privilege to make decisions about the project at hand.

The tool for implementing decisions is often money, so control of the money often indicates who carries responsibility and who holds authority. In addition to following the money, another way to tease apart authority and responsibility is to ask, "Whose decision is this?" and, "Whose job is this?"

This concept has two important applications in the CODOP world. One is in the relationship between a difficult parent and their adult child. The other is in the relationship between adult children of a difficult parent—that is, siblings who share the difficult parent.

When one person has much responsibility and little authority, there is always another person who has little responsibility yet much authority. The person with much responsibility and little authority is virtually guaranteed to be unhappy. They are certain to eventually feel exploited, unappreciated, and disrespected. The person with little responsibility and much authority, in contrast, usually has no complaints at all.

The solution is for the person with more responsibility than authority to inform the person who has less responsibility than authority that the situation is unworkable. She will explain that, if a better balance is not found, she will have no choice but to resign the high-responsibility role. This is certain to get the attention of the other person and open the door to meaningful negotiation.

If your parents are not self-sufficient and in fact rely for their survival on the frequent, even daily, assistance that you provide, then you are indeed earning some authority in return for shouldering this responsibility. There are many instances of healthy mutual aid between older parents and adult children in which the parental home is a financially necessary sanctuary for the adult child and the adult child is a necessary, daily helper to the older parents. This can and should be a mutually respectful and loving situation.

Every adult child of a difficult older parent is an adult, not a child. You have responsibility for yourself. Therefore, you have full authority for yourself. Your parent no longer has the power to judge you, unless you grant your parent that power. If you decide to cancel their power in your head and heart, then your parent's words of opinion are reduced to nothing more than sound waves in the air.

It is a very different situation, however, if your parents are self-sufficient and you are still reliant on them for your financial upkeep. You are not carrying full responsibility for yourself, and therefore have not earned full authority for yourself. Your justification for complaining may actually be very weak. You may need to gratefully endure your difficult parents' behavior as an inseparable companion to their generosity. Your option is to arrange your life so that you are less dependent on a difficult parent for any needs (e.g., money, food, shelter, job, or friends). Each adult child must make their own decision about this. The level of self-sufficiency an adult child shows through their behavior reflects their physical and psychological capacity. We should all strive to be the best we can be.

Concept 10. The intergenerational cascade

"Who we are takes generations to create and doesn't end with death."
—STANLEY SIEGEL

"Being a bad parent is a sign of not having learned from experience."
—MOKOKOMA MOKHONOANA

My patients sometimes give me a look that seems to say, "Do you really mean to say that my parents had parents?! My parents had a childhood?!"

The way we are, our personality, comes from somewhere. Your parent did not just sit down one day and have a new idea to start being selfish, needy, or impossible to please. They became this way because it made perfect sense to them, based on what they had experienced, felt, and observed. In virtually all cases I have seen, the experiences and feelings that most shaped the difficult parent's personality occurred during the parent's own childhood. Yes, your parents also had parents and other significant people...and a childhood of their own! I frequently find that the family history of an adult child of a difficult older parent contains an *intergenerational cascade* of parents and other significant people modeling inadequate social skills, parenting skills, and coping skills. Many of today's difficult older parents faced identifiable risk factors in their own childhood.

How can the child of a difficult older parent come to actually understand their parent? How can they piece together what their parent actually experienced in childhood? How can you discover the factors that influenced your parent to become the person he or she became? Remember, we should assume that everybody does the best they know how to do with their situation. The answer begins with the genogram, described as Skill 2 on page 58.

Ten Insights to Comfort Your Heart

"Understanding requires insight. Insight must be anchored."
—BRIAN GREENE, THE FABRIC OF THE COSMOS: SPACE,
TIME, AND THE TEXTURE OF REALITY

Congratulations on your persistence in finishing the ten concepts above! Let's now shift gears to some ideas that are less academic and more personal and emotional for children of difficult older parents.

Insight 1. Parental love and the CODOP moment

"That's how they say it: He loves you in his own way. Well, what about my way? What if I need for him to love me in my way?"
—TAMMARA WEBBER, BETWEEN THE LINES

"That's all kids want to know—that you love them."
—KIM HARRISON, INTO THE WOODS: TALES
FROM THE HOLLOWS AND BEYOND

Dr. Laura Schlessinger is famously credited with having said that PARENTING is spelled s-a-c-r-i-f-i-c-e. Parents sacrifice their own comfort, wealth, and time, because they love their offspring. I define love, especially parental love, in accord with Scott Peck in *The Road Less Traveled.*

Peck explains that love is a pattern of behavior that reveals a commitment to work for the healthy development of another human being. Difficult parents often do not grasp this. It is no surprise, therefore, that children of difficult older parents live with a pain in their hearts.

If their parent has only recently become difficult, typically from dementia, the pain is relatively small and mainly consists of grief and compassionate sorrow for their parent's decline. If, however, the parent has always been difficult, the adult child's pain goes much deeper. Why? Here are two important reasons.

First, an infant arrives in the world fully equipped and ready to experience love from its caregivers, to receive that love, and to respond lovingly to it. Healthy parents, likewise, greet the baby's birth with joy, and their behavior toward the child is *consistently* attentive, caring, available, kind, and helpful. In this environment, the child thrives.

Parents need not be perfect parents; a child with "good enough" parenting will do fine. In fact, no one has perfect parents, and no one has a perfect childhood. No matter how loving, fair, healthy, and attentive your parents were, there were certainly life skills that come in handy but that your particular background somehow failed to provide you. If you were taught self-reliance, were you also taught generosity and sharing? If you were taught compassion, were you also taught self-respect and the ability to say no? If you were taught assertiveness, were you also taught how to observe and listen? If you were taught gratitude, were you also taught ambition? If you were taught forgiveness, were you also taught how to confront an offender?

Conversely, just as each infant is born fully ready to respond to a loving environment, each infant also arrives in the world fully equipped and ready to perceive a tragic lack of love from its caregivers and environment. It is ready to acknowledge a lack of love and to respond with whatever defensive measures are needed to ensure the baby's daily survival. If, for whatever reason, the parents are *not* attentive, caring, available, consistent, kind, and helpful, the child will, by trial and error, devise adaptations to maintain a tolerable level of emotional comfort in their less-than-ideal world. This is heroic but tragic, because the adaptations are inevitably not ideal for living among the healthier people the child will meet later in life. These adaptations will persist throughout the child's life as scars that can distort their perception of the world and their reactions to the world, resulting in less satisfying relationships.

Second, when these unlucky children grow into adulthood, most eventually grasp that their childhood was distinctly harder than a typical one. They realize that their parent did not embody the normal guiding principles that virtually all people know instinctively regarding how to love, how to parent, and how to be a family. This fact is felt as a very deep betrayal of their parent's basic human duty to their child, thus adding yet another layer of pain for the adult child of a difficult older parent.

We all hold memories of powerful formative moments from our childhoods. Whether they were wonderfully positive or horribly negative, they are moments we will never forget. Every adult child of a difficult older parent has searingly painful memories that I call CODOP moments, because they capture the essence of the difficult traits or habits shown by the difficult parent. For most children, CODOP moments are few and mild. Adult children of difficult older parents share the special burden of frequent and severe CODOP moment memories.

What are your CODOP moments? A helpful exercise for adult children of difficult older parents is to write down the "who, what, when, where" of their CODOP moments. How old were you? Who did what to whom? How did it make you feel? What message did you receive and internalize from experiencing that moment? How did you respond? How did it change you?

Insight 2. Difficult parents have real impact on the child

"When love is unreliable and you are a child, you assume that
it is the nature of love—its quality—to be unreliable. Children do not find fault with their parents until later. In the
beginning the love you get is the love that sets."
—JEANETTE WINTERSON, WHY BE HAPPY WHEN YOU COULD BE NORMAL?

No child of a difficult parent emerges unscathed from the experience. The extent of the painful and unhelpful baggage left inside the child is directly related to how young the child was when the parent began showing difficult behavior. The general rule of thumb is that the younger in the child's life the difficulty began, the more painful, deep, and lasting is the impact on the child's psyche. A person whose parent was normal and pleasant until late life has been spared a raft of possible traumas and should be grateful.

What forms of psychological baggage are commonly carried by adults whose parent has been difficult for decades? There is tremendous variability among these adults, and they range from those who carry virtually no scars to those who suffer chronic psychological pain.

It is common that lifelong adult children of difficult older parents experience below average self-esteem and self-confidence. Instead of developing a healthy view of their difficult parent as a flawed human being, they may swing to either one extreme of agreeing with their parent's negative view of them, or to the other extreme of hating the parent, rejecting the parent's negative view of them, and assuming that most other people are just like their parents. Adults in the first category have difficult trusting their own judgment. They feel less capable than others of functioning effectively in the world, and therefore often place themselves excessively under the influence of others. Adults in the second category have difficulty trusting others, they view others with cynicism, and they resist being influenced.

In both cases, the child's perception of other people is distorted, either in the positive or negative direction. This distortion of other people cannot fail to interfere to some degree in the child's efforts to make friendships, build relationships, and connect heart-to-heart with relatives, or with their ability to appropriately take, give, and share.

If you are an adult child of a difficult older parent, there is tremendous benefit when you invest time and energy into discovering and identifying the specific adaptations you made in childhood and youth to survive your situation. What beliefs did you develop and adopt that helped you make sense of the pain and find an island of peace in the midst of your pain? How well do those beliefs, which were useful at the time, stand up to scrutiny *now*, when you apply your adult knowledge, judgment, and skills?

If you are an adult child of a difficult older parent, there is also tremendous benefit when you fully realize that you are not alone. Unfortunately yet comfortingly, you are in the company of many other truly fine people who also have or had a difficult parent. It is not your fault.

Insight 3. Having a difficult older parent is a personal growth opportunity

"Absence of problems
does not lead to happiness.
Dealing with them does."
—J. BENSON, HAIKU TO LIVE BY: LIFE AFFIRMING
MESSAGES, TO HEARTEN YOUR DAY

A parent with a personality disorder has severe impairment in their ability to love—that is, to demonstrate a commitment to the healthy development of another person. For the adult child of a difficult older parent, loving this parent is a full-time, difficult job. The silver lining is that the hard, scary, and expensive experience of being the child of a difficult older parent is a personal growth opportunity.

The misfortune of having a difficult parent creates a dramatic question for their adult children: "How ready, willing, and able is the child of a difficult older parent to (a) recognize, understand, and master the emotions caused by their loved one's illness, (b) learn new skills, and (c) put in the hard work to master this situation?"

Luckily, the path this growth can take need not be discovered anew by every adult child of a difficult older parent. In my experience, the path typically leads the adult child through six stages, which I call the CODOP response maturation stages.

Stage one is passive, painful victimhood. The child of the difficult parent has no skills for self-protection, no helpful perspective on the parent's behavior, and no hope for relief.

Stage two consists of the child showing ineffective protest, which takes the form of conflict with the parent. This may be episodic or chronic.

Stage three sees the appearance of strengthened but still unsophisticated boundaries established by the adult child. These somewhat block painful attacks, but they also block insight and compassion.

Stage four consists of intentional growth by the adult child based on learning. Through targeted reading and professional consultation, the adult child of a difficult older parent gains greater knowledge, insight, compassion, perspective, and skills. The adult child may now be able to recognize and acknowledge their own contributions to the unhealthy interaction patterns they have with their parents.

Stage five is best described as transcendence. It is marked by the adult child of a difficult older parent now experiencing stable feelings of self-confidence, calmness, and safety, even when in direct interaction with the difficult parent.

Stage six is a focus on legacy and prevention. Here, the adult child not only has mastered healthy parenting skills, but also shows leadership by helping other adult children of difficult older parents recognize their dilemma and their opportunities for personal growth.

Over and above these CODOP maturation stages, adult children of difficult older parents share with all adults the duty to continue maturing psychologically. This maturation is described by psychologists with terms used in two sections above: "coping mechanisms" and "normal aging." In the section on coping mechanisms, it was explained that psychological coping mechanisms like altruism, sublimation, suppression, and humor are clearly preferable to displacement, isolation, repression, or acting out. Psychological maturity is synonymous with using only mature coping mechanisms.

In the section on normal aging, it was explained that maturity includes greater ability to regulate one's emotions. Mature people understand themselves. They know that it is neither necessary nor wise to act upon every emotion. They perceive their own emotions accurately, and they manage their stress. They recognize indicators of emotions in the behaviors of other people, and they have the ability to grasp the perspective of another person. Therefore, they comprehend that person's emotional experience. This allows the mature person to balance the pursuit of their own needs with skills for helping other people experience comfort and success, too.

Having a difficult parent is not an opportunity that anyone would choose for themselves, nor wish upon another person. Nevertheless, it is an amazingly powerful insight that having a difficult parent is ironically a gift, because it is an opportunity for enhanced personal growth. To accept this insight is consistent with such spiritual beliefs as, "God has a plan for my life," "Everything happens for the good," and, "I didn't choose my parents; God chose them for me."

Insight 4. Are difficult parents sick or bad?

This is a hard question. Answering it requires that we also address further questions. Is the parent's difficult behavior unstoppable? Is it an irresistible force, hardwired into them, perhaps directly into their brain tissue? Or is it willful, voluntary, selfish, and malicious misbehavior? Can they stop acting this way? Is their difficult nature an illness or a choice?

The answer is clear in cases of a pleasant parent who turns difficult only after the onset of dementia. This parent is sick.

In the case of the lifelong difficult parent, the answer is elusive. Does the parent warrant a diagnosis of a personality disorder? If so, then illness might be the conclusion. Note, however, that in this realm, illness does not necessarily mean there is no need for punishment. The antisocial personality disorder who is convicted of a felony is not spared prison time or other unpleasant consequences due to a diagnosis. Personality disorders are unique in this regard. The behavior pattern is obviously deviant, yet self-control is still justifiably expected by society and even by loved ones.

Does the answer to these questions of sick versus bad even matter? Yes and no. What matters most is how the individual child of a difficult parent answers the question for himself. His answer strongly affects how much goodwill he can muster for his parent, and how much emotional baggage he carries. A decision to believe the parent is bad leads to less goodwill and more painful baggage. A decision to believe the parent is sick leads to more goodwill and less painful baggage.

Insight 5. Honoring difficult parents

"Honor thy father and thy mother."
—EXODUS 20:12

Everyone knows that the fifth of the Ten Commandments contains the injunction to honor your father and mother. While the Bible speaks of various difficult children, especially sons, there is little precedent there for labeling parents as difficult. I have often challenged myself with the question, "Is it inherently disrespectful or impudent to label a parent's behavior as unacceptable or inappropriate?" Repeatedly, the answer I reach is, "Absolutely not."

How can an adult child of a difficult parent reject their parent's bad behavior while still honoring the parent? The Fifth Commandment gives a clue. The division and structure of the biblical phrases incorporating the Ten Commandments have been the subject of interpretation throughout history, but a popular model divides them into two sets of five and suggests that the first five address man's relationship to God, while the second five address man's relationship to his fellow man. Interestingly, honoring parents is in the first set! This implies that affording even unearned honor to our parents, who gave us life, honors our relationship with God, who gave us life.

Exactly what does the biblical injunction to honor parents mean? What does it require of children? According to many biblical interpreters, the commandment requires that the adult child see to the parent's basic physical needs (e.g., food, clothing, and shelter). It does not require that the adult child love or like the parent, obey the parent's every wish, or submit to abuse of any kind. The parent's safety and dignity are key, not their happiness. The parent must be addressed and treated civilly, but the adult child is not required to endanger his or her own emotional or physical health. Interactions with the parent, when possible at all, should be civil and designed to fulfill at least the minimum requirements of "honoring."

The bottom line is that the child of a difficult older parent can simultaneously honor the parent and use common sense to realistically protect themselves from the toxic aspects of the difficult parent.

In June 2016, I posted my article, "Father's Day: The pleasure & the pain," to my blog. It is included here as an illustration of the special challenge children of difficult older parents face in their effort to balance having a difficult parent against societal pressures to show love toward parents.

Fathers have a powerful and lasting impact on the psychological development of their children, cognitively, emotionally, and interpersonally. Father's Day is a beautiful occasion for honoring fathers who parented in a healthy way. What exactly are the gifts imparted by healthy fathering, and what are the wounds inflicted by unhealthy fathering? Let's looks at three aspects of this (Rosenberg & Wilcox, 2006).

1. Children whose fathers were involved, nurturing, and playful have higher IQs, start school more academically ready, are more patient, and can handle the stresses of schooling more readily than children with less involved fathers. In adolescence, they have better verbal skills, intellectual functioning, and academic achievement.

In contrast, children of fathers who are unavailable, inattentive, or unkind perform worse academically and intellectually.

2. Children who have an involved father are more likely to be emotionally secure, feel confident to explore their surroundings, and, as they grow older, have better social connections with peers. They are less likely to get into trouble at home, at school, or in the neighborhood, and are more sociable and popular with other children throughout early childhood.

Fathers generally do more stimulating, playful activity with children than do mothers. From these interactions, children learn how to control their feelings and behavior. Fathers often push achievement, independence, and an interest in the outside world, while mothers stress nurturing, both of which are important to healthy development. As a result, children who grow up with involved fathers are more comfortable exploring the world around them and more likely to exhibit self-control and healthy social behavior.

Children with good relationships with their fathers are less likely to experience depression, to exhibit disruptive behavior, or to lie. Boys with involved fathers have fewer school behavior problems and girls have stronger self-esteem. Children who live with their fathers are more likely to have good physical and emotional health, to achieve academically, and to avoid drugs, violence, and delinquent behavior.

In contrast, children of fathers who are unavailable, inattentive, or unkind often grow into adults who lack self-esteem, social skills, self-control, and emotional resilience.

3. Fathers influence their children dramatically through the quality of their relationship with the mother of their children. Fathers who have a good relationship with the mother of their children are usually more involved and spend more time with their children, and as a result have children who are psychologically and emotionally healthier. Similarly, mothers who feel affirmed by her children's father and who have a happy relationship are often better mothers.

A positive relationship between mother and father provides vital modeling for children. Fathers who treat the mothers of their children with respect and deal with conflict within the relationship in an adult and appropriate manner are more likely to have boys who understand how they are to treat women, and who are less likely to act aggressively toward females. Girls with involved, respectful fathers see how they should expect men to treat them and are less likely to become involved in violent or unhealthy relationships.

In contrast, research has shown that husbands who display anger and show contempt for or stonewall their wives ("the silent treatment") are more likely to have children who are anxious, withdrawn, or antisocial, and who as adults lack self-esteem, social skills, and emotional resilience, and have more difficulty establishing and maintaining healthy marriages themselves.

The bottom line is that Father's Day is a pleasure for those whose father was loving, but a painful ache in the heart of those whose father was disappointing.

Insight 6. Expectations & satisfaction

"There are two ways to get enough. One is to continue to accumulate more and more. The other is to desire less."
—G.K. CHESTERTON

"He who is not satisfied with a little, is satisfied with nothing."
—EPICURUS

Here is an insight that everyone intuitively feels, but few could put into words until hearing it from another. There is an *inverse relationship between expectations and satisfaction*. The higher our expectations are of ourselves or others, the lower our satisfaction is likely to be. The lower our expectations, the higher our satisfaction is likely to be.

A recent MRI study found evidence for this in brain functioning. Dr. Robb Rutledge and his team at University College London studied twenty-six healthy men, ages 20–40. Their findings were published in the *Proceedings of the National Academy of Sciences* in 2014. They had participants perform a probabilistic reward task in which they chose between certain and risky monetary options while being asked after every few trials to report, "How happy are you right now?" All the while, the subjects' brain activity was monitored with an MRI brain scanning machine. Both self-report and brain activity records indicated that positive expectations reduced the positive emotional impact of trials with positive outcomes, and negative expectations reduced the negative emotional impact of trials with negative outcomes. In other words, we are not disappointed when we expect and receive little, nor overly exuberant when we expect and then receive the reward. The researchers also developed a smartphone app that paralleled the study using points rather than money. Data from over eighteen thousand participants with the app replicated the laboratory findings.

Does this mean we should abandon ambition and never "aim high"? Should we abandon all efforts to strive for greatness or reach for improvement in our lives and in the lives of those we seek to lovingly influence? This is a tough question. As Jeremy Sherman (2014) wrote in *Psychology Today*, "Have higher expectations if you want improvement and lower expectations if you want contentment. If you want to get bigger and encourage others to get bigger, cultivate high expectations even if it means being disappointed or sounding uncompassionate, and if you want to feel big enough already and satisfied with what others deliver, lower your expectations."

A closely related psychological concept is called primary control vs. secondary control. Basically, *primary control* refers to the steps we take to directly affect our world, to create or avoid some real situation in the real world. When we get sick, we find the right doctor and ask him to take concrete steps to make us well. When the roof leaks, we get the roof fixed so the leak will stop.

Secondary control, in contrast, refers to our ability to adjust our beliefs and emotions about a situation after discovering that the specific desired outcome is impossible to achieve. If we don't have enough money to buy the car of our dreams, we buy what we can afford and talk ourselves into being content with it. If we lose in love, we grieve and say it was all for the best. Secondary control is a righteous and time-honored defense mechanism.

It is useful to know that the distinction between primary and secondary control, essentially the difference between fighting and accepting, is rooted in our brain anatomy. Our brain structures include areas that together are called the autonomic nervous system (ANS). The ANS contains two circuits, each of which is activated automatically under certain conditions. One circuit is called the parasympathetic nervous system. When activated, it produces the fight-or-flight response, in which the body is put on high alert for rapid extreme action. In the modern world, where sabre tooth tigers rarely invade our caves, this response now takes the form of anxiety, worry, and insomnia. The other ANS circuit is the sympathetic nervous system. When activated, it produces relaxation and acceptance, and often sleep. For us, this takes the form of peaceful coexistence with things we cannot change.

Finally, it is very useful to have an objective standard against which to compare our expectations for happiness. Many scientific studies involving hundreds of thousands of respondents have demonstrated that, in developed countries, there is a roughly "u-shaped" curve of happiness across the adult life span. That is, from a relatively high level of happiness around age eighteen, contentment gradually falls, reaching a low point in our forties. Thereafter, the average happiness level gradually rebuilds, reaching a lifetime high in our sixties, and then drifting slightly downward again. There is substantial evidence for this finding, both from studies that look at people of all adult ages in one period of time and from studies that choose a large panel of respondents and question them repeatedly across the decades.

The same type of happiness research is often applied to the issue of marital happiness. The results here, too, yield a reliable u-shaped curve. Here is how happiness in the "average" marriage proceeds. Partners are happy as newlyweds. The birth of the first child is associated with a dramatic drop in marital bliss, and it remains quite low until the children are all "out of the nest." At this time, there is a robust rebound, and couples at this stage report very high levels of marital satisfaction.

The lesson from these research findings on marital and general happiness in adulthood is clear. Every adult faces many demands, frustration, responsibilities, challenges, and losses. Adulthood is not a vacation, but rather it is hard work. Adults must therefore be realistic and not expect uniformly happy years.

Insight 7. Adult duty to be logical and realistic

"The standards of judgement must be rooted in the whys
and wherefores of life as it is lived, the world as it is, not
our wished-for fantasy of the world as it should be."
—SAUL D. ALINSKY, RULES FOR RADICALS: A
PRAGMATIC PRIMER FOR REALISTIC

Perhaps the greatest challenge in treating personality disorders is that the difficult individual does not recognize their behavior is a problem. They lack insight. They blame others for relationship problems, for their unhappiness, and for the disapproval they experience from others. Their long track record demonstrates that they either cannot or will not learn to see themselves more objectively and change their behavior. After all, when was the last time you heard a difficult person say, "I've decided to go into psychotherapy to work on my personality disorder"?

The only path to a more peaceful life for the child of a difficult older parent is to change *himself*. "But wait!" you might say. "Whose fault is it that I am a child of a difficult older parent, and whose responsibility is it to fix the situation? I'm not the sick or crazy one! Why not just get help for my parent? Why do *I* have to change? Why is it up to me to do all this work?!"

This is a profoundly important question. The answer is that is it virtually impossible to change another adult's personality. Only they can change themselves, and then only with intention, hard work, commitment, and professional help. This rarely happens. This means that people remain who they are, unless they mindfully and effectively work at changing themselves.

Difficult people, including parents, will continue to be difficult. It is unrealistic to think otherwise, and adults have a duty to be realistic. Everyone has thoughts or beliefs as well as feelings. Thoughts and beliefs should obey the rules of logic, while feelings, alas, are usually free from such constraints. I like to use the image of a bus as a metaphor for a person and ask this question: "Who will drive this bus—my emotions or my logical, adult, objective side?" To deny or reject reality is to choose emotions over facts. I contend that adults have a duty to keep their logical side in the driver seat.

Being realistic includes acknowledging that certain dreams, yearnings, and hopes can never be fulfilled. Children of difficult older parents are often plagued by impossible hopes that their mom or dad will finally become loving, attentive, and appreciative. This hope is unfounded in most cases. The sad truth is that the child's dream of having healthy, loving parents and a mutually satisfying relationship with them is already dead. The child of a difficult older parent must let such dead dreams die.

The child of a difficult older parent who repeatedly expresses amazement, shock, or surprise at Mom's or Dad's latest outrageous or difficult behavior has not accepted this insight. Surprise at yet another unpleasant act is clearly not justified. How is surprise possible, after such a long track record of similar behavior? Quite simply, surprise reflects denial and a lack of acknowledgment that the hope and dream of a healthier parent are dead.

Indeed, as in any death, for the child of a difficult older parent, there is much to grieve. The situation includes so many losses involving the impaired loved one: their health, their intelligence, their abilities, their broken personality, their companionship, the good that might have been, etc.

Another clear indication that a child of a difficult older parent has not understood this insight is when the child continues to try to change their parent's personality or behavior. Given the impossibility of changing another person, the only rational choice left to the adult child is to *let people be who they are*. Their parent is going to be who they are no matter what we do, so we may as well accept it.

The child of a difficult older parent begins maturing when she stops being surprised at the thousandth replay, begins to let dead dreams die, begins grieving this loss and all the other losses, and begins letting people be who they are. This is realism. This is healthy adulthood.

Insight 8. What about my *other* parent?

"My dad had limitations. That's what my good-hearted
mom always told us. He had limitations, but he meant no
harm. It was kind of her to say, but he did do harm."
—GILLIAN FLYNN, GONE GIRL

In my experience, it is rare to have two difficult parents. Thankfully, one
difficult parent is by far the norm.

As children of difficult older parents work with me to deepen their
toolbox, the conversation often turns to important questions about the
other parent. "Why didn't he protect me?" "How could my dad not know
what this woman was like before marrying her?" "Through the years,
didn't Dad know what we kids were experiencing at the hands of our
mom?"

The fact that the difficult parent was married means that the non-
difficult parent also had a difficult spouse. Although they typically chose
this life partner and married with genuine expectations and hopes for a
happy life together, the non-difficult spouse learned at some point that
their hopes for happiness would find limited fulfillment. In some sad
cases, the non-difficult spouse knew before the wedding that their future
spouse was a difficult, unpleasant person, and that unhappiness lay ahead.
Yet they proceeded with the wedding.

Here is the most common scenario I have seen in these marriages.
The non-difficult spouse discovers that the difficult spouse is strongly re-
sistant to reasonable efforts to change her behavior to be more pleasant.
Any such efforts, in fact, are met with vicious punishment from the unpleasant spouse. In some cases, the non-difficult spouse is rather passive.
Due to their temperament and their lack of skill, this spouse is unable
to mount any serious effort to counter the difficult spouse's challenging
personality. In extreme cases, especially with an unpleasant husband, the
non-difficult spouse is a wife who is frankly submissive and dependent.

Soon, the pleasant spouse retreats in defeat. Husbands will spend
the minimum necessary time with the family and find other arenas for
relaxation, acceptance, validation, and pleasure. This may be golf, cards,
business, alcohol, or any other distraction. On rare occasions, it may
be investing in the children. More often, however, the children are left

behind emotionally, as the non-difficult parent seeks peace outside the home. Wives more often, in my clinical experience, hunker down for decades of fruitless attempts to placate their difficult husband. The children are trained in her methods for placating their difficult father.

What options, choices, or freedom of movement did the non-difficult spouse or parent have in order to improve the situation? In 20/20 hindsight from a twenty-first century perspective, it is easy to say that divorce was an obvious option—and perhaps the best option. We must remember, however, that today's older adults probably first married around 1965. This was before the summer of peace and love, before women's liberation, before the sexual revolution, before divorce was liberalized, and just one year after the passage of the Civil Rights Act created the U.S. Equal Employment Opportunity Commission. These individuals carried the mindset of pre-1965 America with them as they travelled through their adult years. Personal choices for individuals in unhappy marriages were, or at least felt, far more restricted than they feel for today's non-elderly adults.

Insight 9. Forgiveness

> "An apology means nothing if they don't stop doing what they're apologizing for. Believe action, not words."
> —MANDY HALE

Difficult parents did or do not treat their children as well as the children deserve or deserved. For this unfairness, is it ever appropriate or possible for the child of a difficult older parent to forgive the parent?

No one is perfect. It is an inescapable part of life that people sometimes make mistakes. Luckily, there are some social mechanisms that (a) allow people to repair the damage caused by their bad behavior, and therefore (b) allow social relationships to return to a healthy, fulfilling state. Together, these mechanisms are called forgiveness.

In philosophical terms, forgiveness is an example of the apparent dichotomy of justice versus mercy. From a strict justice standpoint, a wrongdoer must be held accountable for bad deeds by suffering some unpleasant consequences. This is thought to teach the wrongdoer as well as observers that they must not commit bad acts again. From a mercy point of view, we empathize with the wrongdoer and imagine they did wrong only due to some overwhelming situation that may have caused any of us to do likewise. We also speculate that the wrongdoer is already remorseful and has already learned their lesson. Therefore, actual punishment is unnecessary and perhaps even cruel.

In either viewpoint, the end goal is a wholesome society filled with psychologically whole individuals. What should be the pathway to healing that addresses both the justice aspects and the mercy aspects of the situation?

One widely adopted mechanism for forgiveness focuses on the aggrieved party or victim. This approach strongly urges the victim to forgive the damaging party. It is seen as a desirable, God-like character trait for the victim to forgive the perpetrator. The victim who does not forgive is considered less mature than the victim who does forgive. This approach focuses heavily on mercy and compassion.

Another model puts responsibility for the victim's forgiveness on the perpetrator. This model insists that forgiveness is readily available but must be at least partially *earned* through performance of some specific steps, some of which are behavioral and some of which are psychological. This approach strives to balance fairness and justice with mercy and compassion.

The specific steps for earning forgiveness would include:

1. Admission of wrongdoing.
2. Acceptance of responsibility.
3. Acknowledgement of harm; empathy for victim's suffering or other distress; Remorse, regret ("I am sorry.").
4. Explanation of what happened and why.
5. Sincere offer of prompt and full repair/compensation/restitution ("How can I make this up to you?").
6. Promise to behave better; forbearance ("I promise nothing like this will ever happen again.").
7. Request for forgiveness.

Taking both of the above models into account, one sees that regardless of perpetrator's actions, the victim has options. The victim can:

1. Indefinitely retain a vivid memory of the offensive behavior, maintain their conscious disapproval, anger, and resentment, and make repeated demands for restitution and punishment.
2. Release their demands on the perpetrator and cancel the debts, but retain their disapproving opinions and feelings. This compromise approach often includes gently and lovingly confronting the perpetrator and constructively communicating the effect of the perpetrator's actions on the victim.
3. Relinquish rights to all negative feelings and all demands for consequences and nurture undeserved compassion, generosity, mercy, and even love toward perpetrator.

How does this apply to difficult older parents and their adult children? In my experience, difficult parents remain difficult and do not engage in serious efforts to earn forgiveness. Therefore, their adult children are faced with choosing from the short list of options shown above. Notice that the three choices span the continuum from pure justice to pure mercy. Concepts and insights discussed in this book that can assist the child to consider #3 include recognition and sympathy for how parents' personalities were formed (Concept 6 on page 27), and discovery of the intergenerational cascade (Concept 10 on page 34).

Insight 10. Transmission prevention (CODOP STOP)

"How can it be, after all this concentrated effort and separation, how can it be that I still resemble, so very closely, my own detestable mother?"
—GABRIELLE HAMILTON, BLOOD, BONES, AND BUTTER: THE
INADVERTENT EDUCATION OF A RELUCTANT CHEF

In one of my CODOP community meetings, we went around the circle and allowed each of the mostly female participants to introduce themselves and their situation. The lone male attendee introduced himself as simply accompanying and supporting his wife, who was a child of a difficult parent. In the course of the meeting, however, I mentioned that more than one male child of a difficult older parent in my practice had described his father as a "dream killer." With this, the male group member started crying. I asked him what was happening. He replied that his father was exactly like that, and furthermore, he suddenly realized that he had behaved the same way toward his own children.

My CODOP program and this book are dedicated to easing suffering in the present and in the future. It is supremely important that today's children of difficult older parents dedicate themselves to creating a healthy legacy for their own children by exhibiting healthy parenting behaviors. Today's child of a difficult older parent is free to choose between (a) remaining trapped by their baggage and their damage, or (b) taking their future and their family's future into their own hands and steering their behavior to a healthy direction.

Modern civilization on earth has dedicated enormous resources to eliminating many scourges that have plagued mankind since antiquity, and many successes have been achieved. Smallpox, polio, and malaria are all but extinct. My macro-scale vision is that unhealthy parenting will one day also be only a memory on earth.

On the micro-scale, building a healthy legacy requires that individual children of difficult older parents look deeply into themselves for the courage to relinquish revenge and find compassion for the difficult parent. It requires that children of difficult older parents commit themselves to breaking the toxic intergenerational cascade. It requires that children of difficult older parents learn how normal, healthy families behave with each other, and then practice those healthy behaviors. The ten skills outlined in the next section will help you do this.

Ten Skills to Guide Your Actions

"The brain is your emotional cockpit. Lots of buttons and levers. Best to learn how to steer responsibly."
—LISA CYPERS KAMEN, ARE WE HAPPY YET?: EIGHT
KEYS TO UNLOCKING A JOYFUL LIFE

In this section, I recommend specific actions and behaviors, even specific words, for children of difficult older parents as they refine their approach to their parent or to their parent's impact on them. Building on the concepts and insights described previously, these skills are where the rubber meets the road. They are the final common pathway, the actual behaviors that my patients have repeatedly found improve their situations.

Skill 1. CODOP self-care

"By loving you more, you love the person you are caring for more."
—PEGGI SPEERS, THE INSPIRED CAREGIVER: FINDING
JOY WHILE CARING FOR THOSE YOU LOVE

Being a child of a difficult parent can be extremely challenging, even brutal. It can be lonely, heartbreaking, exhausting, and demoralizing. It is bad enough that a difficult parent creates emotional pain in the adult child, but the extension of the harm to include physical health consequences must be prevented. Therefore, the first step in CODOP self-empowerment is adopting healthy self-care habits.

These include a healthy diet, frequent exercise, minimal alcohol use, and adequate sleep. The list also includes socializing with and confiding in healthy friends and relatives, carefully managing the time spent with the difficult or impaired relative, and maintaining your own schedule of medical checkups and care.

Relating to a difficult parent, especially when the situation is compounded with caregiving, is really hard. You must take care of yourself to survive and succeed.

It is essential to recognize that self-care is not selfish. In fact, the child of a difficult older parent who most strongly wishes the best for their challenging relatives will be the most committed to self-care. Why? Because the difficult relative needs their child's help. If the child of a difficult older parent neglects self-care and allows himself to burn out as a caregiver, the older parent will lose an irreplaceable helper. There will be no one to offer the social, psychological, and practical safety net the difficult parent often needs. In short, self-care is altruistic, not selfish, because if the child of a difficult older parent burns out, the parent is more likely to "crash and burn" as well.

For example, Stan's mother, now seventy-two, had always been high maintenance. She had ruled the roost when Stan and his sister, Claire, were young. Later, she still managed to reach deeply into Stan's and Claire's relationships and break up both of their marriages. She remained abusive toward both Stan and Claire, but Claire found a way to move to a distant city, leaving Stan to look after Mom. He certainly had his hands full, since she called him at least twice a day with some complaint or demand.

Stan, now forty-six and single, did his best, but it was never enough for Mom. If she called him at 2:00 A.M. saying she heard a noise and feared she had an intruder, Stan rushed over to check every room and then rest on her couch until she fell asleep. His job performance the next day was terrible, but what could he do? Mom then ridiculed him for his meager salary and his failure to advance in his career. Once, he was offered a better job at a higher salary, but it would require being out of town one day each week. When he told his mom about the offer, she was horrified. How could he even consider leaving her "alone" so often? On the rare occasions Stan met a lady and begun a friendship, his mom expertly planted doubt in his mind about the lady, accused him of selfishly wanting to abandon his mother, and created "crises" that interfered with his outings with the lady friend. The friendships did not last.

In our sessions, I helped Stan understand that his mother was showing poor judgment by causing him trouble in the romantic, financial, and physical health areas of his life. She was causing damage to the most valuable person in her world. Her well-being depended totally on his well-being. Therefore, the best way for Stan to ensure her well-being over the long term (that is, the best way to love her) was to take better care of himself. His mother may not want him to do this, but she needed him to do this. This gave Stan the strength to restrain his excessive availability to his mom and more fully meet his own needs for privacy, income, sleep, leisure, and friendship.

Skill 2. The genogram

"Roots are, I'm learning, as important as wings."
—MICHELE HUEY

A powerful method for systematically exploring your parent's lifetime of experiences that surely contributed to their personality is to compile their family tree into a one-page diagram called a genogram. A genogram is a drawing that shows all of a person's relatives and other closely involved individuals, with detailed notations about the personality of each person.

The genogram has a vocabulary of its own. Males are represented by a square and females by a circle. Marriage is a horizontal line with little upturned lines at the end, each end touching the bottom of a circle or square. For non-marital relationships such as a romance or creating a child, the horizontal bracket is made of dashes rather than a solid line. Offspring are placed an inch or two below the line linking parents, and a vertical line connects each offspring to the parental bracket (not to an individual parent). Siblings are shown in birth order, from left to right, each with a single vertical line connecting them to their parental pair. Twins each have a line touching the same spot on the parental bracket, creating an upside-down V. Earlier generations are thus located higher on the

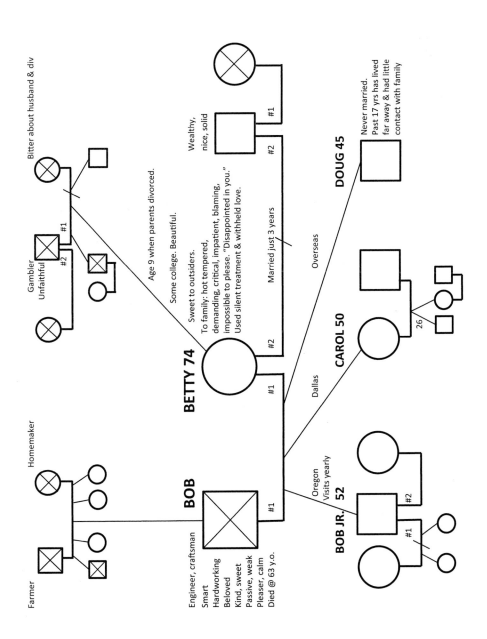

page, and more recent generations are lower on the page. I find it helpful to place the difficult parent, and his or her entire generation, about half-way down the page.

Once all the related individuals are represented in the diagram, the psychological inquiry begins in earnest. Notes are written next to each circle or square indicating the leading characteristics of the individual's personality. The notes might say, for example, "Calm, hardworking, kind," or "Passive, giving, reliable." Or they may say, "Impossible to please, screamer, harsh." Whatever is the truth should be written down.

With this one-page family tree in hand, it becomes possible to detect any trends or patterns. Was there someone in the parent's young life who modeled unpleasant behavior? Was the parent the target of unpleasant behavior? Were they fortunate enough to receive adequately mature parenting, or were their parents absent, distracted, self-absorbed, damaged, abusive, intoxicated/addicted, or overwhelmed by illness, poverty, violence, dislocation, prejudice, or other misfortune?

Creating the genogram makes it possible to begin finding answers to these fundamental questions.

Skill 3. Emotional fluency

"We live at the level of our language."
—ELLEN GILCHRIST

"The limits of my language are the limits of my universe."
—JOHANN WOLFGANG VON GOETHE

Emotional fluency can be compared to language fluency. Language fluency includes many composite skills, such as reading, writing, spelling, vocabulary, and mastery of the parts of speech, the tenses and voices of verbs, the number, gender, and case of nouns, and grammatical rules for constructing meaningful and effective sentences.

Similarly, emotional fluency includes: having a vocabulary for the many emotions; the ability to detect emotions in ourselves and others; skills for processing and appropriately expressing both pleasant and unpleasant emotions and helping others do the same, etc.

Psychologists actually have a fancy name for the inability to know or name one's emotions. It is *alexithymia*. Boosting your emotional vocabulary by learning the names of feelings is a basic but necessary skill that will better equip you to solve your CODOP dilemma. How many names of emotions do you think you could write down right now? Give it a try. If you run dry after naming about ten, take a look at this book's appendix, where you'll find over 250.

Note that people often unknowingly miss an opportunity to clearly identify their current emotion. Specifically, when asked the question, "What are you feeling?" they give an answer that begins, "I feel that..." The words that follow are a thought or belief, not an emotion. The necessary follow-up question is, "What emotion are you feeling?"

As the appendix illustrates, there are many overlapping names for emotions. There are two related emotions that are highly relevant for children of difficult older parents, which many people erroneously consider to be synonymous. They are **guilt** and **regret**. CODOPs often describe feeling guilty for not feeling more love, joy, or enthusiasm about their parents and the relationship. When asked, "Exactly what do you mean by this word, guilt?" they usually answer that they "feel bad about it."

It is common and natural that children of difficult older parents describe this bad feeling as guilt. Everyone has been taught from birth to "do the right thing" and "honor and obey your parents." Guilt is the shame or remorse that one feels upon realizing that one has broken a rule, done something wrong, or done something they should not do. So feeling guilty makes sense in that the child of a difficult older parent is not fulfilling the global obligation of cheerful obedience that parents implant in young children.

But is being unable to find joy in enduring a difficult parent's obnoxious behavior really breaking any rule? Where is it written that we are obligated to feel love for someone who is mean to us? In actuality, the child's feeling of guilt ("I should be doing more") reflects the child's loving and well-meaning, but actually unfairly harsh, self-blame.

In contrast, the emotion that does stand up to adult scrutiny is regret ("It is a darned shame this is happening, but it is not my fault"). Regret is a much less onerous emotion to bear than guilt.

After guilt and regret, a third key emotion children of difficult older parents must understand is **grief**. Grief is the normal, healthy, appropriate, and usually temporary sadness we feel when we realize we have lost something we love or treasure. As mentioned in Insight 7 on page 48: Adult duty to be logical and realistic, children of difficult older parents yearn for a parent who is healthy, pleasant, and capable. In fact, the child of a difficult older parent continues to hope their parent will become these things despite years or decades of not being so. There is always room for hope that anyone might change their chronic behavior patterns for the better—but one's estimate of the likelihood of such a change should be realistic. To be overly hopeful is irrational and can border on denial. When the child of a difficult older parent opens her eyes and stops denying her parent's nature and likely future behavior patterns, she will have to grieve the dead dream of having healthy, loving parents anytime soon.

A fourth key emotion for children of difficult older parents to process is **anger**, including resentment. It was and is completely unjustified, undeserved, and unfair that the child of a difficult older parent did and does endure rude and hurtful behavior. It can be extremely tempting to strike back against this maltreatment with aggressive words and deeds. Children of difficult older parents often suffer a painful inner conflict about these urges toward their own parents.

A fifth key emotion for children of difficult older parents to process is **gratitude**. As difficult as being a child of a difficult older parent is, life could always be worse. If your parent was emotionally abusive, was she physically abusive, too? If you hungered for love, approval, and encouragement, did you also hunger for food? There is always something to be grateful for, in addition to the terrible things that make us angry and hurt. Being a child of a difficult older parent might even have a silver lining. How would you be different if your parents were within the normal range and pleasant? Would you be only better, or in any way worse? These are all questions with which children of difficult older parents grapple at some point.

In my psychotherapy work, I frequently pose the question, "How do you feel about that?" Quite often, my patient answers, "I don't know." I have discovered that patients assume that this response is an end of the inquiry. It is a new concept for them when I explain that "I don't know" is not the end of the discussion, but only the beginning of the deeper exploration into their psychological life.

For example, Seth, a forty-nine-year-old child of a difficult parent, had a chronically difficult father who, despite Seth's specific requests to the contrary, sometimes gave inappropriate gifts of money to Seth's children. I asked Seth how he felt about this. When he answered, "I don't know," I explained to Seth that it is perfectly OK to not know what he was feeling...yet. I then explained further that his next step should be to slow down, look inside, and see if he couldn't find some possible or partial piece of the answer to the question. If Seth could find within himself any tiny bit of the answer, it would mean that he would already understand himself better than before.

Seth took some slow breaths and silently looked inside himself, and then realized that he could indeed name the emotions his father's behavior caused. These included anger, humiliation, and resentment. Seth was then also able to link these emotions to memories of his boyhood interactions with his dad, in which his dad similarly dismissed Seth's preferences and his efforts to develop his own identity.

As Seth's example illustrates, the work of the child of a difficult older parent to master their challenges cannot succeed without learning some vocabulary for emotions.

Skill 4. Boundaries

> "'No' is a complete sentence."
>
> —ANNE LAMOTT

A boundary is a rule about what contact or access one person will allow another person to have with or to them. What will I allow another person to know about me, to see of me, to hear from me, or to say or do to me? How much of my time will I allow them to occupy, and at what time of day or night? When will I allow them to see or speak with me? What part of me, my home, my belongings, or my family will I allow them to see, touch, have, or control? It is up to me to answer and establish rules about all of these questions.

Boundaries should be consciously designed, implemented, and enforced. Boundaries should be communicated or announced with words, and they must be given reality by imposing negative or unpleasant consequences when the rule is violated. The consequence need only be mild and gentle as the rule is being learned, but it must be more substantial or distressing if rule violations continue or grow.

A closely related concept to boundaries is assertiveness. People vary greatly in their style of exerting influence on others and accepting influence from others. These styles fall on a continuum, stretching from passivity on one end to assertiveness in the middle and finally to aggressiveness.

Passive individuals accept influence from others as commands. They follow others' wishes obediently and neglect their own preferences in life. The goal of passive behavior is to please others. Few passive individuals are fully content. Their wishes are seldom fulfilled. They usually harbor growing feelings of resentment, which periodically manifest in the form of aggression or anger.

At the other extreme, aggressive individuals forcefully strive to impose their preferences on others. Their goal is to control and dominate others. They disregard both others' rights to enjoy their own preferences and others' unpleasant feelings when the aggressor fails to respect those preferences. Aggressive people are experienced by others as unpleasant.

Passive-aggressive individuals employ a confusing, hybrid approach to influencing people. They show behaviors that are harmful to others, yet they hide behind a veil of deniability of responsibility for their behavior's harmful effects on others. For example, a homemaker wife may allow her executive husband to run out of clean shirts on the very morning of his big meeting, and then claim the oversight was unintended or due to unforeseeable circumstances. Likewise, the working wife may find that her husband has "unintentionally" left her car with an empty gas tank on the morning of her big meeting. A pattern of such behavior generally reflects distinctly negative emotions, such as anger or resentment, that the person does not want, or feel able, to acknowledge and own.

Assertiveness is by far the preferred style. Assertive individuals are motivated by a desire to be known and to understand others. Through word and deed, they communicate clearly to others what they want for themselves and what they expect of others, as well as what they are and are not willing to do. Assertive individuals respect the rights and preferences of others, and they negotiate in a courteous spirit of mutual respect. When necessary, they can say that the item at hand is NOT their problem. They speak in polite and business-like tones, without sarcasm or recrimination. To be assertive is to consistently communicate in a way that is both clear and firm, and constructive and respectful. Assertiveness leads to greater contentment for the individual and more pleasurable interactions with others.

When relating to difficult people, maintaining healthy boundaries takes on special importance. One specific and important boundary is to guard your own important personal information. Children of difficult older parents should be very careful about sharing information with the difficult parent. It will be used against you. Another specific boundary is your time management. Remember that the adult child of a difficult older parent has total unilateral authority to reduce or minimize the time they spend in visiting, giving assistance to, or worrying about the difficult parent.

For example, Brian, a thirty-year-old bachelor, was moving back to his hometown to take a new job. On a preliminary visit, he rented an apartment and made arrangements for his furniture and accessories to be moved into his new home. He planned to arrive in town with a full week free for unpacking and setting up his place. His mother, who had always been overbearing, desperately wanted to "help" her son. She begged Brian repeatedly for a key to the apartment, because she wanted to arrange his furniture and hang his pictures. She declared dramatically how much she would enjoy doing this for him, implying that he owed her this pleasure.

Brian, who had had considerable counseling regarding his difficult mother, knew that he must enforce his personal boundaries with her or risk an avalanche of invasions by her into his life. So, every time his mom begged for the keys, Brian responded calmly and pleasantly, "Thank you so much, Mom. That is very kind of you, but I will be doing that myself. I have some ideas that I want to experiment with, and I will need to be there myself to make these decisions." When his mom repeated her pleas, Brian simply repeated his answer. Mom finally relented. In this way, Brian not only resolved this challenge. He delivered a message to his mom that he was now his own man. He had behaved assertively, neither passively nor aggressively, and he had established a firm and healthy boundary.

Skill 5. Become a smarter fish

"Turn your wounds into wisdom."
—OPRAH WINFREY

"Good judgment comes from experience, and experience comes from bad judgment."
—RITA MAE BROWN, ALMA MATER

Difficult people, be they a parent, a spouse, a sibling, an in-law, or a not-so-young child, are adept at provoking loved ones into arguments that are invariably as pointless as they are painful. To help people learn to avoid being "hooked" by their difficult person's provocations, I frequently share the visual image of a wise older fish looking at a fisherman's nearby lure with skepticism. The bait looks juicy and delicious, but the smart fish knows there is a hook hidden within, and he lets the bait simply float away. I urge my clients to become smarter fish. I remind them that smart fish remain alive to swim around and grow old, while not-so-smart fish are easily hooked and wind up on the fisherman's dinner table. Children of difficult older parents should strive to ignore inaccurate or provocative questions, accusations, or statements. Otherwise, they will find themselves repeatedly hooked.

A closely associated skill is to stop being surprised. As discussed in Insight 7 on page 48. Adult duty to be logical and realistic, children of difficult older parents must learn to stop being surprised at their parent's actions. There must be an end to surprise! Children of difficult older parents must learn to recognize the same old patterns of behavior in their difficult parent. They should know by now what is coming next. The parent really is predictable. The script is well-known. The job of the child of a difficult older parent, then, is to choose to never again enact their same old part in the same old play. Smart fish do this by choosing to not swallow the bait.

For example, Laura's ever-critical mother had a habit of rolling her eyes at Lisa, indicating condescension and disapproval. In Laura's life, this eye roll had triggered hundreds of bitter fights. Mom's expert eye roll, so subtle and effortless, was also very effective at hooking Laura into a painful frenzy of emotion. Every fight consisted of Laura vehemently defending herself against her mother's implied criticism.

At the end of a recent visit to her mom, Laura said, "I'll see you soon, Mom," and Mom responded with a roll of her eyes, a disbelieving wrinkle in her brow, and a sideways twist of her mouth. Laura, right on cue, took immediate notice and offense, and she responded with a full voice, "What's *that* supposed to mean?! I just spent half the day with you! We had a perfectly nice lunch, but it is never enough for you, is it?! What do you want from me?!" Laura had swallowed the bait and now was a hopelessly hooked fish. When Laura finally walked to her car after fifteen painful minutes of argument, she was completely worn out and depressed.

Once Laura learned her CODOP skills and became a smarter fish, she came to respond to provocations like this much more calmly. Now, after Mom's eye roll, she says with a smile, "I know. You'll believe it when you see it, right?" and heads straight out the door. Or she simply ignores the expression and heads out the door with a wave and smile. She takes great satisfaction in having become a smarter fish.

Skill 6. Avoid pointless confrontation with irrational people

"You cannot reason people out of a position that
they did not reason themselves into."
—BEN GOLDACRE, BAD SCIENCE

Difficult people routinely seem to disregard the rules of logic when interpreting the world and interacting with others. If they don't like something which you consider right and proper in the world, the difficult person might actively criticize and resist it, loudly and often. In dementia, emotions are contagious, and in personality disorders, the actions and words of others are often misperceived. Rational discussion about the matter has no apparent effect on their beliefs, feelings, or actions. This can be extremely frustrating for the child of a difficult older parent.

In these cases, my clients have invariably worn out two common but useless approaches. The first is reasoning, that is, explaining why you are right and they are mistaken, explaining why you wish they would behave differently, asking them to behave differently next time, or revealing how their behavior makes you feel. The second is confrontation, such as demanding that they change or threatening some consequence if they do not change.

Both of these strategies rely on an assumption that the loved one respects and uses logic in their own thinking and decision-making. But they don't think logically, so these strategies fail. I am often tempted to ask the question famously attributed to TV's Dr. Phil, "How's that working for you?"

I teach my clients a powerful two-part strategy for avoiding confrontation with irrational people. The first ingredient is to remain vague and noncommittal about facts. Do not say yes; and do not say no! Say things like, "Oh!" "Interesting!" "You don't say!" "Isn't that something?" "Wow! Let me check on that," and, "I don't know." The second ingredient is to use your words to express your empathy for their feelings. "That must be hard," and "What's that like for you?"

Finally, it so happens that a simple, three-word phrase powerfully combines these two elements of vagueness and empathy. It is, "I hear you!"

Using this strategy is a conscious departure from how we behave with rational people. It is a bold effort to finesse the difficult, irrational individual away from a pointless and painful interaction. The strategy will only succeed if it is implemented with conviction. It requires a degree of acting skill, as all elements of your delivery must be convincing and sincere. The tone and volume of your voice, the pace and timing of your words, and the expressions on your face must all be congruent with the message. The subtlety and skill required here is similar to driving a car through an icy neighborhood. Each element and step must be planned in advance and delicately executed.

For example, Clint often visited his elderly dad with moderate Alzheimer's disease, who lived in a secured memory care unit. During every visit, dad angrily insisted that, at the end of this visit, he was leaving with Clint, returning to his own home, getting into his car, and driving to Kansas City to visit his parents. Clint repeatedly explained that the home had been sold and Dad was now living there because he has memory problems. Clint reminded his dad that he needed help and he was not safe at home. Clint further explained that Dad's parents are long dead, Kansas City was fifteen hundred miles away, the car had been sold, etc., etc. This never went well, since Dad disputed every fact Clint cited.

As Clint learned his CODOP skills, he learned to avoid these pointless confrontations with his irrational father. Now, when his dad says, "Now, don't you try to leave here without me today. I'm going home to get my car, and you can't stop me, you hear me?!" Clint responds, "Yes, sir, I hear you!"

Dad: "How is my car? Is it gassed up and ready to go?"

Clint: "That's a good question. I haven't seen it in a while."

Dad: "What do you mean, you haven't seen it? It's right there in our driveway, isn't it?"

Clint: "It could be. I've been so busy lately, I'm afraid I haven't looked." Then he'd add, "I'm really sorry about that, because I know how important this is to you. That Buick has always been a great car, hasn't it? A real pleasure to drive, and a beauty, too."

Clint then redirects Dad somewhat: "By the way, Dad, remind me about how you came to buy that car. Wasn't the salesman related to your poker buddy, Bill? What ever happened to those guys?"

It can be very hard to resist the temptation to reason with someone, but if you have a loved one who does not respond to reasoning or confrontation, give this recipe a try. Remember, often in life, less is more!

Vague & Empathic Responses

COMPLAINTS / CRITICISMS

1. I see!
2. Amen!
3. I hear you.
4. Wow!
5. You don't say!
6. Very interesting!
7. Isn't that something?
8. Good point!
9. I'm glad you told me about this.
10. Thank you for telling me!
11. That must be hard for you.
12. That makes sense to me!
13. That's really frustrating (or aggravating), isn't it?
14. Tell me more about that.
15. What's that like for you

QUESTIONS

1. That's a good question!
2. I don't know.

REQUESTS / DEMANDS

1. I will sure look into that.
2. This is important.
3. It will be great if we can work this out.
4. Let's make this happen.

PRESSURE TO ACT IMMEDIATELY

1. As soon as I can.
2. This is just for now.
3. I'm going to try to do this as soon as possible.
4. I'm not sure when.
5. I can't promise when, but I hope very soon.
6. Would it be OK if I call you soon with an update?

Skill 7. The therapeutic fib

"In human relationships, kindness and lies are worth a thousand truths."
—GRAHAM GREENE

Children of difficult older parents should not let a naive commitment to total honesty blind them to the difficult person's emotional idiosyncrasies. A person with a personality disorder may *look* like a regular person who will acknowledge the truth, respect facts, and obey the rules of logic. In reality, however, they will not! They cannot, because their internal life is ruled by their emotions, not by truth, facts, and reality. Likewise, dementia sufferers almost universally are impaired in their ability to be logical. Therefore, since *they* are not constrained by the truth, *you also* must be free to bend the truth when necessary for their and your well-being. It is often totally appropriate to bend the truth to reduce the victim's resistance to necessary care. This is called the "therapeutic fib."

For example, imagine that your mother with clearly documented dementia insists that you give her the car keys or take her to get her license renewed. Mom *wants* to have access to driving, but she *needs* to *not* have access to driving. It is totally loving and appropriate to tell a small untruth about the car being "in the shop waiting for incredibly expensive repairs," or "The computer system at the department of motor vehicles is broken, so they can't process renewals now." When mom asks, "When will this get fixed?" your answer should be vague. You'll say, "Soon, I hope." Or perhaps you'll say that the doctor says she can't drive. When mom asks, "For how long?" you'll answer, "Just for now, until you get better." "Well, when is that going to be?" You'll say, "Soon, I hope." "For now" and "soon" are very useful answers in many situations, because they keep hope alive. For now and soon are therapeutic fibs.

If these words shock you, you are not the first. My patients often respond, "You're just teaching me to manipulate my parent!" or, "Isn't this just lying?!"

Words like *manipulate* and *control* are loaded terms. They are really just polite ways to accuse someone of bullying, exploiting, or abusing. More loaded still is the word *lying*. Every child is appropriately taught that lying is universally wrong. The fact that social tactfulness involves daily small lies ("You look great today!") is somehow never recognized as proof that lying is *not* universally wrong. As a result, some children of difficult older parents who first learn about the therapeutic fib will insist that it is "just wrong to lie" and will therefore feel guilty using the technique.

In fact, influencing another person can be and usually is totally righteous. When we teach, or give advice, guidance, or feedback, it is all influencing. When we visibly or verbally respond to a healthy person's deeds with pleasure or displeasure, gratitude or disappointment, attraction or revulsion, approval or rejection, we are intentionally providing meaningful feedback with the power to influence that person's future deeds and behavioral choices. This is as it should be. We all serve as mirrors to those around us, reflecting back to them the quality and impact of their actions. This is how we learn.

So, you can call this process anything you want. I call it influence, and I like to assume that everyone's motivation for providing feedback or input to others is benign or even constructive and loving. If a healthy person is acting badly and we point it out to them or respond unappreciatively to it, this is wholesome and deserved. Of course, when we give feedback to others and use other methods of influence on them for purely selfish motives, then perhaps verbs like *control, manipulate, exploit*, and *abuse* are appropriate.

When the person in question is unable to make appropriate use of honest feedback, the legitimate, loving, and more effective approach is to finesse them into behaving better through such strategies as the therapeutic fib. I believe that good people who might view the situation impartially would all agree with the wholesomeness of this approach.

For example, Clint, whose dad kept insisting that Clint take him out of the memory care unit, made good use of the therapeutic fib to help his dad be content and cooperative.

Clint: "Dad, I'm so sorry I forgot to tell you the latest news about your car. The last time I saw it, it had a big oil stain under it. It needs to go to the mechanic. Let me do this. As soon as I can, I'll get on it. We certainly need to make sure it is road worthy. Give me a few days and I'll know more about it."

Dad: "Well, I sure hate to wait."

Clint: "Right!"

Dad: "You be sure to let me know right away."

Clint: "Right!"

Dad: "I expect to hear from you tomorrow!"

Clint: "Right!"

Dad: "You call me first thing in the morning, got it?"

Clint: "Right! That's my plan, Dad. But right now, I got to get going. Love you, Dad. Bye."

Dad: "Bye, son. Thanks for helping me out with the car."

Skill 8. Seek out and accept support

"Giving feels fantastic and for there to be a Giver, there must be
a Receiver, so allowing yourself to receive is an act of love."
—REBECCA O'DWYER

Have you recently said "aah"? I hope you have. Think of a cool drink
on a hot day. Even my three-year-old granddaughter knows that "aah"
means happiness, relief, pleasure, and comfort. Do you know what "a-a-
h" stands for? I didn't know either, until it came to me one day. It stands
for (and I'll stick by this forever) "ask for and accept help." Of course!
What brings happiness, relief, pleasure, and comfort better than asking
for and accepting help? Not much!

Why are so many people reluctant to do so? Here in Texas, and
probably all over America, there is a widespread ethos of rugged self-
reliance, which holds that an honorable person takes full responsibility
for oneself, stoically endures the consequences of one's own decisions,
and views asking for help as weakness or failure.

I certainly agree that it is desirable that everyone dig deeply into
themselves for courage, perseverance, effort, and skill to move their life
forward and contribute to society rather than selfishly exploit its resources.
At the same time, we know that life often hands people extraordinary
challenges that quickly overwhelm one's normal coping resources. Is it
good for society for that person to crash and burn? Is it honorable to let
unfortunate circumstances grind people down from strained to crushed?
I don't think so.

Regardless of a general ethos of rugged self-reliance, there are circumstances in which good judgment requires asking for and accepting
help. That is, the rules change! To adhere to the usual rule when the
rules should change is stubborn, unwise, selfish, and self-destructive. This
truth is widely represented in adages such as, "If you want to go fast, go
alone, but if you want to go far, go together," or, "It takes a village," or,
"There, but for the grace of God, go I."

Do not be secretive with friends and family about your difficult parent. Hiding their behavior and its impact on you protects your parent
from the natural consequences of their behavior. This is called enabling.

In other words, your secrecy may be actually creating more bad behavior in your parent.

The alternative to secrecy can be called "going public." I recommend that children of difficult older parents inform their healthy friends and relatives of their challenge of having a hard-to-love loved one. The reality of being a child of a difficult older parent, while tragic, is certainly not shameful. The light of day is therapeutic. Any embarrassment usually quickly evaporates as the child's new confidants respond with acceptance and support. The odds are that they actually knew all along, but were waiting for the child of a difficult older parent to speak up.

When you get a toothache, do you do your own dental work, or do you visit a dentist? When you or a loved one is suffering acute or prolonged emotional upset, do you Google it, or do you consult a psychologist? To reach "a-a-h!" remember to ask for and accept help.

For example, Jeff and his father, Harold, worked together in a successful insurance agency started by Harold's father decades ago. Harold was a consummate businessman and salesman who had made his father proud and had happily taught everything he knew to Jeff, his only child. Harold had made a lot of money during his career. He and his wife lived in a beautiful and expensive home, and his wife had never had to worry about a thing. Harold took care of everything for her, and they were happy.

At age sixty-eight, Harold still went to the office daily and carried full authority. However, Jeff started noticing his father making small but uncharacteristic errors in his work, errors that Harold himself did not notice. In addition, Harold started showing emotional reactions that were uncharacteristic for him, such as sarcasm toward male employees, inappropriate comments to female employees, and irritability with customers. His personal grooming became less fastidious, and his punctuality, which had always been perfect, became less reliable.

Staff started looking uncomfortable around Harold in the office and began asking Jeff questions. Jeff minimized their concerns and told them everything was fine. Then customers whose accounts Harold had handled for years started calling Jeff to fix Harold's mistakes. One big customer moved their coverage to another agency. Despite all this, however, on most days, in most areas, and with most people, Harold was fine. He remained greatly respected and highly visible in the local business community and in his church. Jeff and his mom told everyone that everything was fine.

But Jeff and his mom also took Harold to the doctor. After extensive evaluations, the doctors returned a diagnosis of frontal lobe dementia. This is a progressive brain disease that impairs judgement first and eventually memory. Harold was in the early stage, but it was inevitable that it would gradually get much worse.

Jeff began quietly paying more attention to his father's finances, and what he discovered rocked his world. Harold was secretly in debt, having fallen into the grasp of con artists over the previous two years. He was sending tens of thousands of dollars to "Amy," a Taiwanese "girlfriend" he had never met except on the phone, to support her and her "child." Jeff discovered an envelope full of letters and emails from her, as well as photographs of her and her child. They all proclaimed their love for him, and their gratitude for sustaining them through one tragic financial crisis after another. The envelope also contained letters from certain "relatives" and "friends" of Amy's, whose tone was less friendly. These messages were more threatening, explaining that Harold had a responsibility to Amy, who now loved him, to never break her heart or abandon her, or else terrible things might happen to Harold and his family in the US.

Upon uncovering this mess, Jeff and his mother at first were ashamed of Harold and kept the matter secret from everyone they knew. How, they reasoned, could they possible ruin Harold's sterling reputation, after his decades of hard work and clean living?

In our sessions, however, I helped them see that, in fact, the *only* way to honor his sterling record was to indeed go public. It was exactly his brain disease that rendered him vulnerable to both the obviously shady initial come-on that he fell for and the further lies that trapped him in this web of criminal exploitation. Jeff and his mother proceeded to explain Harold's disease to relatives, friends, employees, and customers. Every one of these people expressed relief to learn this logical explanation. They all also expressed sincere solidarity with Harold's family as they began the sad journey of his decline. Most surprising for Jeff and his mother were the two people who, upon learning about Harold's situation, revealed that they had similar situations in their families and now had the courage to reach out for support, too.

Skill 9. Dementia-specific care strategies

"While no one can change the outcome of dementia or Alzheimer's, with the right support you can change the journey."
—TARA REED, WHAT TO DO BETWEEN THE TEARS...A PRACTICAL GUIDE TO DEALING WITH A DEMENTIA OR ALZHEIMER'S DIAGNOSIS IN THE FAMILY

"Caregiving will never be one-size-fits-all."
—NANCY L. KRISEMAN, THE MINDFUL CAREGIVER: FINDING EASE IN THE CAREGIVING JOURNEY

It has been my experience that parents who have been difficult for decades generally cause more psychological distress than parents who were pleasant until developing dementia in later life. For this reason, most of this book has addressed children of long-difficult older parents. There are, however, specific caregiving skills that are essential in dementia cases which are not always relevant in CODOP situations without dementia. Let's take a look at those now.

First, it is important to clarify some fundamental *goals* for the adult whose parent is newly difficult due to dementia. Here are two I consider vital. The first is to give the parent a pleasant journey through their years with dementia and provide a graceful exit at the end. The second is for the caregiver to stay healthy and to grow personally through the caregiving experience.

Let's now look at effective care strategies in three core domains: communication, behavior, and mood in the dementia sufferer.

Communication

The caregiver must acknowledge that the sufferer's progressive brain dysfunction impairs language ability. Therefore, the usefulness of conversation and words unavoidably shrinks. This gives actions and behavior more and more importance.

A core caregiving strategy regarding communication is for caregivers to reduce reliance on spoken language and become fluent in comprehending behavior. Caregivers should speak in simple words with short messages, and go one step at a time. Link words to behavior by presenting both simultaneously.

A second core caregiving strategy regarding communication is to frame questions wisely, and be careful what you ask for. That is, be careful how you ask for it. When you want your confused parent to do something, do not ask, "Do you want to…?" Rather, give them the choice between two options that are equally acceptable to you. "Would you rather take a shower or a bath?" Don't give them the chance to say no.

Behavior

Caregivers must remember that progressive dementias cause a person's abilities to degrade and disappear. This first impacts complex behaviors and eventually impacts simpler behaviors. Generally, the simpler behaviors are mastered earlier in life, and complex behaviors are mastered later in life. The more complex self-care skills, like cooking, driving, and managing money and medications, deteriorate earlier, in early dementia. More basic self-care skills, like eating, bathing, dressing, and toileting, deteriorate in mid-stage dementia.

There are several core caregiving strategies regarding behavior:

- First, remember that only behavior matters! The sufferer's need for assistance, and the help they receive, need not be spoken about at all with the parent. Distract the sufferer with words, but elicit the desired behavior through actions. "Speak" to the victim through your behavior.
- Second, prompt the sufferer to the toilet every two hours when awake.
- Third, provide the amount of help needed, not much more and not much less.
- Fourth, provide activity support. Dementia robs its victims of the ability to independently think of, plan for, and carry out activities. All of their planning and preparation needs to be done for them.
- Fifth, praise and thank the victim a lot; try to never scold or say no.

- Sixth, create structure through a routine, stable schedule that is predictable yet also re-calibrated as needed. Provide support consistently, to prevent the sufferer's needs from getting ahead of the amount of help given.
- Seventh, "feed and water" the victim frequently every day.
- Eighth, completely remove any guns from the home.

Mood

Caregivers must remember that dementia sufferers regress in their emotional maturity. Their tolerance for frustration weakens month by month. For dementia sufferers, emotions are contagious. That is, if the frustration they are unintentionally causing in their caregiver results in the caregiver showing irritability to the dementia sufferer, the dementia sufferer's behavior will become irritable as well. It is up to the healthier member of this dyad to stop this toxic spiral.

These five core strategies can help you manage a dementia sufferer's mood:

- Minimize the patient's frustration. Be as attentive and reliably available as possible.
- Check frequently for physical discomforts such as being hot, cold, hungry, wet, soiled, or in pain.
- Avoid confrontation by using the formula described in Skill 6.
- Give reassurance, praise, and appreciation. Keep hope alive.
- Strive to always be calm, pleasant, and cheerful.

For example, Phyllis's always-sweet mother, Irene, began experiencing progressive cognitive decline around age sixty-three. It was accompanied by unpleasant personality changes. At first, Irene's occasional episodes of irritability, forgetfulness, poor judgment, crude language, thoughtlessness, and trouble finding places when driving left Phyllis surprised, confused, and irritated. After Irene was diagnosed with Alzheimer's disease, Phyllis understood better, but she was still frustrated by Irene's inability to benefit from reminders and her lack of remorse for her socially inappropriate behaviors.

When Phyllis first visited me, she was facing many painful feelings, including frustration, grief, fear, and guilt. She also reported having frequent arguments with Irene. For example, Phyllis would discover during her nightly visit that Irene was not following the posted schedule to use the toilet, and she was hiding her wet underwear under her mattress or in the pantry. Phyllis, exasperated, would remind Irene to go to the toilet at the times posted on the refrigerator door. Irene would insist she didn't need that silly list. Phyllis would cite the facts. Irene would take offense. Phyllis would feel hurt and insist she was just trying to help. And so on.

During our sessions, Phyllis took to heart all of the strategies mentioned above for maintaining Irene's mood and behavior. Phyllis learned to not expect Irene to remember anything said to her or to pay attention to any written notes. A caregiver was hired to stay with Irene, first during the day and later around the clock. Phyllis reduced her visit frequency a bit. I helped Phyllis provide the caregiver with a list of activities that Irene found interesting but doable, activities that were simplified as Irene's abilities declined.

Phyllis and the caregiver established for Irene a stable daily routine incorporating grooming, nutrition, toileting, rest, and activities both at home and outside the house. Phyllis and the caregiver practiced using vagueness about facts and empathy about feelings to avoid pointless confrontations with Irene. Together, these strategies created a largely calm lifestyle for long periods of time for all three women.

Skill 10. Overcome difficult behaviors in yourself

"There is nothing noble in being superior to your fellow man; true nobility is being superior to your former self."
—ERNEST HEMINGWAY

"You are essentially who you create yourself to be and all that occurs in your life is the result of your own making."
—STEPHEN RICHARDS, THINK YOUR WAY TO
SUCCESS: LET YOUR DREAMS RUN FREE

No one knows better than a child of a difficult older parent how painful and unfair it is to suffer with a difficult parent. Thus, no one should be motivated more than a child of a difficult older parent to not be a difficult parent themselves. I urge children of difficult older parents to work at being the very best person they can be in relation to their children. That is, to work at being the kind of person and the kind of parent they always wished their difficult parent would be.

How is this done? It simply requires you to learn to show *more* of the traits and behaviors on the *left* side of the table below in your family relationships, and *less* of those on the *right* side. Easy, right? Of course not! It takes real effort, real attention, and real commitment to improve ourselves. But isn't this really our only job in life?

As we go about this self-improvement project, it is important that we not rely solely on our own opinions about our progress. We might be just a little biased! Rather, we must solicit feedback from loved ones with questions like:

- "How am I doing?"
- "What is it like having me as a wife, husband, mom, or dad?"
- "Is my company enjoyable?"
- "How can I improve?"
- "How can I better show how much I like, love, enjoy, and respect you?"
- "How can I help you and others like, love, enjoy, and respect me more?"
- "How can I help you be the best you can be?"
- "What are your goals in life, and how can I help you accomplish them?"

More	Less
Assertiveness	Aggressiveness, passivity
Authenticity*	Hypocrisy, dishonesty, two-facedness
Patience, tolerance, tact	Criticism, cynicism
Giving the benefit of the doubt, judging favorably	Blaming, judging negatively
Kindness	Sarcasm
Encouragement	Belittling
Listening	Talking, lecturing
Respect for boundaries	Intrusiveness, pushiness
Gratitude, appreciation	Entitlement, demands
Humility	Pride
Empathy	Callousness
Smiles	Scowls
Openness to feedback	Arrogance, self-righteousness
Self-control for words & deeds	Impulsivity, thoughtlessness
Focus on healthy development of others	Focus on others' usefulness to you.
Giving, effort	Irresponsibility, helplessness, selfishness

*Congruence between your private and public selves; congruence between your beliefs, your words, and your deeds.

For example, Shawn and Doris married in their late twenties and are now in their later forties. Their three children are teenagers. Doris's mother and Shawn's father have both always been difficult individuals, so both Shaun and Doris carry emotional scars from their childhoods. Shawn's father passed away just two years ago, but Doris's mother is still living and difficult. Doris had several consultation sessions with me to master my CODOP concepts, insights, and skills.

The crowning accomplishment that Doris wanted to work on was to protect against giving her children and husband the same sort of toxic experience with her that she and others had had with her mother. Her specific steps toward this goal began with reviewing and understanding the guidance in the More/Less table above.

Her next step was to invite her husband, and later her kids too, to give her feedback on her behavior and her personality, as they experienced it in their interactions with her. She asked them to schedule a time to sit down with her for an hour, in a quiet place and without interruption. She began each meeting by thanking them for agreeing to meet with her. She then asked them for honest feedback, using the questions mentioned above. She listened calmly and respectfully. She even took some notes. She thought of their feedback as a precious gift of knowledge from the mouths of people who were experts on *her*. She frequently asked them to pause so she could paraphrase their comments back to them, to make sure she understood them correctly. She would say, "I think what I hear you saying is..." She would follow the paraphrase with, "Did I get that right, or is there something I need you to clarify for me?" Doris did not speak one word of self-defense or self-justification, and of course not one word criticizing the speaker. At the meeting's end, she again thanked them and told them she loved them and would do all she could to use the feedback constructively. The meetings caused her husband and kids to all feel much closer to Doris, and more loved by her, than they had before.

Inspired by his wife's commitment to not replicate her mother's mistakes, Shawn later asked Doris and their children to sit down with him and give him feedback, too.

PART THREE

Implementation

"Play ball!"

—BASEBALL UMPIRE

Action Trees for the Top Twelve Difficult Parent Scenarios

Thirty tools are a lot to master at once. Although I hope every reader will study all thirty carefully and repeatedly, I want to also provide a jump-start to readers whose CODOP dilemma is too acute and pressing for extended study before taking action. Alternatively, once you have read through this brief volume at least once, let me suggest what are usually the most valuable tools for children of difficult older parents in each of the following six classic difficult parent scenarios.

1. INTRUSIVENESS refers to the parent who arrives at your home or office uninvited and then stays too long, ignoring normal social indicators that their visit is ill-timed. They may phone you too often and routinely try to pry into your private topics during conversation. They show up at your kids' sports events and push their way into your conversations with your friends.

The main tool for children of difficult older parents in this scenario is *managing boundaries assertively* (Skill 4 on page 64). A boundary is a rule about what contact with us, or access, we allow another person to have. Boundaries should be consciously designed, implemented, and enforced. Assertive individuals communicate clearly to others, through word and deed, what they want for themselves and what they expect of others, as well as what they are and are not willing to do.

2. LAZINESS refers to the parent who is needy yet uncooperative. In many instances, they warrant the label of a "help-rejecting complainer." They neglect the management of themselves and their home. When the child of the difficult older parent generously tries to help in these tasks, the parent is passively obstructionist and unappreciative. The help of the difficult older parent's child is blocked or undone, and the complaining continues.

The main tools for children of difficult older parents in this scenario are *becoming a smarter fish* (Skill 5 on page 67), *understanding the meaning of honoring parents* (Insight 4 on page 40), *and understanding authority vs. responsibility* (Concept 9 on page 33).

Becoming a smarter fish is my description of methods for ignoring inaccurate or provocative questions, accusations, or statements by responding with vagueness about facts and empathy about feelings.

The Bible's Fifth Commandment, "Honor your father and mother," does require that the adult child see to the parent's basic physical needs (e.g., food, clothing, shelter, etc.), but it does not require that the adult child love or like the parent, and it does not require that the adult child obey every wish of the parent or submit to abuse of any kind. The highest goal of the difficult older parent's child should be protecting the parent's safety and dignity, not necessarily their happiness.

Responsibility refers to doing the work, putting in one's own money, time, or effort, and generally "carrying the load" for a certain project, such as caring for an impaired relative. Authority is the privilege to make and enforce decisions about the project at hand. If you are ever asked to accept, or have the thought on your own to take, responsibility for a project that you are not also given adequate authority to complete, my advice is don't do it!

3. BLAMING, CRITICISM refers to the parent who is unappreciative, crassly disrespectful, and hateful. This parent has a history of actively disparaging your character to your face and to others. As far as this parent is concerned, you never do anything right. Your accomplishment and assistance are dismissed or taken for granted, and all you hear from the parent is criticism.

The main tool for children of difficult older parents in this scenario is *avoiding pointless confrontation with irrational people* (Skill 6 on page 69). Because difficult people routinely disregard the rules of logic when interacting with others, rational discussion often has no beneficial effect on their beliefs, feelings, or actions. Reasoning and confrontation both repeatedly fail to bring about peace or agreement. I recommend that children of difficult older parents use a two-part strategy in conversation with the difficult parent. This consists of (a) being vague and noncommittal about facts and (b) expressing empathy for the parent's emotions.

4. DISHONESTY: refers to the parent who lies to you and others, betrays your confidence, reveals your secrets, and gossips about you and others. This parent does not hesitate to bend or break the truth to serve their convenience, win them social points, or protect their pride.

The main tools for children of difficult older parents in this scenario are *managing boundaries assertively* (Skill 4 on page 64), *choosing appropriate guiding principles* (Concept 8 on page 31), *and seeking help/going public* (Skill 8 on page 75).

First, a boundary is a rule about what contact with us, or access to us, we allow another person to have. Boundaries should be consciously designed, implemented, and enforced. Assertive individuals communicate clearly to others, through word and deed, what they want for themselves and what they expect of others, as well as what they are and are not willing to do. This has broad application with dishonest parents.

Second, children of difficult older parents must decide which principles will guide their behavior toward their difficult parent. The traditional option with healthy parents and with healthy adults in general is to prioritize their autonomy, that is, their right to full disclosure of information relevant to them and their right to make all of their own decisions in life. The main alternative, which applies to the degree that the parent is not healthy or competent enough to handle the consequences of their own poor choices, is to prioritize the parent's *safety and dignity* above their autonomy.

Third, going public to seek out and accept help is a valuable skill for children of difficult older parents. The light of day has the ability to discourage dishonesty. Going public is difficult for many, however, because it conflicts with such feelings as pride and privacy. Having a parent who lies can be embarrassing, until the child of a difficult older parent understands it as more of a tragedy than a shame. I have found that embarrassment quickly evaporates as the new confidants of the difficult older parent's child respond with acceptance and support. Often, the friends actually knew all along about the difficult situation with the difficult older parent's child, but were waiting for the child to speak up.

5. IRRESPONSIBILITY refers to the parent who squanders their own or their child's resources and accepts no accountability for their actions. This parent has poor judgment, foolishly trusting the untrustworthy stranger and expending no effort to protect themselves from exploitation. They spend excessively, impulsively, and selfishly. Either through addiction to "sweepstakes" or having naively fallen into a web of con men and scams, they are being systematically separated from their money. Yet they refuse to accept guidance from their children that they are being scammed.

The main tools for children of difficult older parents in this scenario are *achieving realism* (Insight 8 on page 51), *choosing appropriate guiding principles* (Concept 8 on page 31 and described above at Dishonesty), *and understanding authority vs. responsibility* (Concept 9 on page 33 and described above at Laziness).

Adults have a duty to be realistic. This includes acknowledging that certain dreams, yearnings, and hopes can never be fulfilled. The sad truth is that the child's dream of having healthy, loving parents and a mutually satisfying relationship with them is already dead. The child of a difficult older parent must let such dead dreams die. Surprise at new examples of the difficult parent's pattern must eventually give way to acknowledgment of and grief over the tragedy of the situation.

6. INNOCENT FAÇADE refers to the parent who treats everyone else much nicer than they do their own child. Few or none of their friends have ever seen the parent behave meanly to you, and therefore would find it difficult to believe your description of your parent's difficult behavior. This parent presents a misleadingly pleasant face to the public and creates a private hell for the child. The parent's hypocritical, two-faced behavior leaves the adult child constantly wondering which persona is their parent's authentic one. The child's normal lifelong instinct and desire to trust the parent is chronically and perversely blocked by the outwardly normal parent's cruelly disapproving treatment of their child.

The main tools for children of difficult older parents in this scenario are *lowering your expectations* (Insight 5 on page 43) *and seeking help/going public* (Skill 8 on page 75, described above at Dishonesty).

It is a fundamental psychological fact that there is an inverse relationship between expectations and satisfaction. The higher our expectations are of ourselves or others, the lower our satisfaction is likely to be. The lower our expectations, the higher our satisfaction is likely to be. If we are willing to tolerate disappointment in our pursuit of difficult goals, that is certainly fine. However, if the likelihood of success is low and we will suffer unbearable disappointment upon failure, we should probably be prudent and trim our expectations. With difficult parents, it is unsustainable to expect them to suddenly change their longstanding behavior pattern. Lowered expectations are called for.

What are the most valuable tools for children of difficult older parents in the cognitive six difficult parent scenarios, which are found in parents who have become newly difficult with the onset of dementia? These six are repetitiveness, restlessness, wandering, delusions, anger/aggressiveness, and depression/withdrawal.

The primary strategies for these are concentrated in Skill 9 on page 78, Dementia-specific care strategies. These include framing questions wisely, using distraction, toileting every two hours, providing activity support, maintaining a stable activity routine, avoiding unpleasant emotions, checking frequently for physical discomfort, providing frequent snacks and hydration, and, perhaps most vitally, avoiding pointless confrontation.

Identifying the most valuable tools for children of difficult older parents in the cognitive six difficult parent scenarios is a more concise task than the foregoing discussion of the classic six scenarios. For all six scenarios (repetitiveness, restlessness, wandering, delusion, aggression, and depression), the full menu of strategies is required. In my opinion, however, the single most powerful dementia-specific tool for optimizing a dementia sufferer's behavior and mood, thus minimizing all forms of difficult behavior, is activity support. Among the other tools discussed in this volume, the next most powerful tool for optimizing a dementia sufferer's behavior and mood is avoiding confrontation.

Closing Thoughts

Congratulations! Through investing your time in reading this book, you have acquired thirty powerful tools, including ten concepts to empower your mind, ten insights to comfort your heart, and ten skills to guide your actions. You are growing! Your mastery of these growth strategies positions you to make meaningful progress through the CODOP response maturation stages. By applying them, you can improve yourself, your life, and the lives of those you love. As promised in the Introduction, you now *know* the ten concepts, *realize* the ten insights, and are ready to *practice* the ten skills.

I want to leave you, however, with just a few very important thoughts.

The role of psychological consultation

Are you the kind of person who does your own taxes, paints your own rooms, changes your car's oil, and homeschools your children? Outstanding! You are confident and multi-talented and enjoy mastering new skills.

Do you also perform your family's dental work yourself and make your own shoes? I suspect not, because success at these tasks requires a suite of specialized tools, knowledge, and experience that you do not possess and don't have the time or opportunity to acquire. Therefore, you turn to experts for such services.

Being a child of a difficult older parent can fall anywhere along this spectrum. If the thirty tools presented here suffice to move you along the CODOP maturation path as far as you want to go, I am thrilled. However, if you find yourself stymied and can't progress further on your own, you owe it to yourself and your children to enlist the help of a properly trained mental health professional. Being stalled is probably not caused by you, but by the difficulty of your particular CODOP situation. There is no shame in making use of the right resources to accomplish your goal. In this sort of consultation, you control the number and frequency of sessions. Often, even one session can dramatically improve your focus and direction.

Your courage, your future

The motivation you have shown by reading this book is the motivation that will keep you working until you master your dilemmas as they arise. Of course, you have more reading to do, and the resource list that you will find below is an excellent place to start. And remember, you can always contact me directly and schedule an individual consultation. I would welcome the opportunity to work with you.

I am very optimistic about your eventual success. Have courage. You are growing. I believe in you. I have faith in you, and I am proud of you already!

Your invitation to engage further with me

I am passionate about CODOP, and writing this book has been a labor of love. However, I consider this just the beginning.

The CODOP program is taking many forms, including (a) building a mutually supportive community of children of difficult older parents in Dallas, (b) raising awareness of CODOP through public presentations and dissemination of this book, and (c) teaching both the public and the mental health community the concepts, insights, and skills that will allow children of difficult older parents to thrive, in Dallas and beyond.

You can help in this effort by sharing with or recommending this book to others, proposing me as a speaker at appropriate speaking venues, and directing others to the "Grow Into It" blog on PaulKChafetz.com, where every second post is about CODOP.

I am eager to stay in contact with every reader. Here are some ways we can do this. You are invited to:

1. Visit and explore my *website*, PaulKChafetz.com.
2. While there, visit the *blog* page and read about CODOP and other topics I have addressed.
3. On the *blog* page, click the *subscribe* button to add yourself to my blog notification list.
4. On my website, visit the *media* page and listen to some of my *podcasts* on many interesting psychological topics.

5. On my website, complete one or more of the *self-assessments* I have created to support your psychological growth.

6. Join my *Dallas CODOP group* on the website Meetup.com, and attend whenever possible. This website will keep you up to date about my speaking schedule.

7. Contact me about arranging a *personal psychological consultation* in my office for yourself or someone you know who has a difficult older parent. If you or they live in Texas but not in the Dallas area, the consultation can be done via Skype, Facetime, etc.

8. Contact me about *speaking* to your organization.

9. Contact me about being your *guest in your media venue*, such as radio, television, magazine, newspaper, blog, podcast, etc.

10. Contact me about coming to your city and conducting a *workshop* about CODOP for your organization.

APPENDIX: 250 EMOTION NAMES

abandoned
acceptance
adoration
affection
aggravated
agitated
aggressive
alert
amazed
ambitious
amused
anger
animosity
annoyed
anticipation
anxiousness
appreciative
apprehensive
ardent
aroused
ashamed
astonished
attraction (sexual, intellectual, or spiritual)
awed
betrayed

bewildered
bitter
bliss
blue
boastful
bored
breathless
brokenhearted
bubbly
calm
camaraderie
cautious
cheerful
cocky
cold
collected
comfortable
compassionate
concerned
confident
confused
contempt
content
courageous
cowardly
crafty

crazy
cruelty
crushed
curious
cynical
dark
dejected
delighted
delirious
denial
depression
desire
despair
determined
devastated
disappointed
discouraged
disgust
disheartened
dismal
dispirited
distracted
distressed
down
dreadful
dreary

eager	greedy	left out
ecstatic	grief	liberated
embarrassed	grouchy	lively
emotional	grudging	loathsome
empathic	guilty	lonely
emptiness	happy	longing
enchanted	hate	love
enigmatic	heartbroken	lovesick
enlightened	homesick	loyal
enraged	hopeful	lust
enthralled	hopeless	mad
enthusiastic	horrified	mean
envy	hostile	melancholic
euphoric	humiliated	mellow
excited	humored	mercy
exhausted	hurt	merry
expectation	hysterical	mildness
exuberance	indignation	miserable
fascinated	infatuation	morbid
fear	infuriated	needed
flabbergasted	innocent	needy
foolish	insecure	nervous
frazzled	inspired	obscene
frustrated	interest	obsessed
fulfilled	intimidated	offended
furious	irate	optimistic
gay	irritated	outraged
giddy	jaded	overwhelmed
gleeful	jealous	pacified
gloomy	joy	pain
goofy	jubilant	panicky
grateful	kind	paranoia
gratified	lazy	passion

pathetic

peaceful

perturbed

pessimistic

petrified

pity

playful

pleased

pleasure

possessive

pride

provoked

proud

puzzled

rage

regretful

relief

remorse

resentment

resignation

resolved

sadness

satisfied

scared

Schadenfreude

scorn

selfish

sensual

sensitive

sexy

shame

shocked

shy

sincerity

solemn

somber

sorrow

sorry

spirited

stressed

strong

submissive

superior

surprised

sweet

sympathetic

temperamental

tense

terrified

threatened

thrilled

tired

tranquil

troubled

trust

tormented

uncertainty

uneasiness

unhappy

upset

vengeful

vicious

warm

weary

worn-out

worried

worthless

wrathful

yearning

zest

REFERENCES & RESOURCES

1. Balkin, R. S., Freeman, S. J., & Lyman, S. R. (2009). Forgiveness, reconciliation, and *mechila*: Integrating the Jewish concept of forgiveness into clinical practice. *Counseling and values*, 53, 153-160.

2. Bernstein, A. (2001). *Emotional vampires: Dealing with people who drain you dry*. New York: McGraw Hill.

3. Brown, E. (1999). *Living successfully with screwed-up people*. Grand Rapids, MI: Revell.

4. Cade, E. (2002). *Taking care of parents who didn't take care of you: Making peace with aging parents*. Center City, MN: Hazelden.

5. Carstensen, L. L., Isaacowitz, D. M., & Charles, S. T. (1999). Taking time seriously: A theory of socio-emotional selectivity. *American Psychologist*, 54 (3), 165-181.

6. Cohen, S. S., & Cohen, E. M. (1997). *Mothers who drive their daughters crazy: Ten types of "impossible" moms and how to deal with them*. Rocklin, CA: Prima.

7. Farmer, S. (1989). *Adult Children of Abusive Parents: A Healing Program for Those Who Have Been Physically, Sexually, or Emotionally Abused*. New York: Random House.

8. Forward, S. (1989). *Toxic parents: overcoming their hurtful legacy and reclaiming your life*. New York: Bantam.

9. Forward, S. (2013). *Mothers Who Can't Love: A Healing Guide for Daughters*. New York: Harper.

10. Halpern, H. (1990). *Cutting Loose: An Adult's Guide to Coming to Terms With Your Parents*. New York: Simon & Schuster.

11. Lebow, G., & Kane, B. (1999). *Coping With Your Difficult Older Parent: A Guide for Stressed-Out Children*. New York: Harper Collins.

12. Neuharth, D. (1998). *If You Had Controlling Parents: How to Make Peace With Your Past and Take Your Place in the World*. New York: Harper Collins.

13. Peck, M. S. (1978). *The Road Less Travelled.* New York: Touchstone.

14. Prager, J., & Glaser, M. (2016). *100 Years: Wisdom From Famous Writers on Every Year of Your Life.* New York: W. W. Norton.

15. Rosenberg, J., & Wilcox, W. B. (2006). *The Importance of Fathers in the Healthy Development of Children.* U.S. Dept. of Health & Human Services. https://www.childwelfare.gov/pubPDFs/fatherhood.pdf

16. Roth, K., & Friedman, F. (2003). *Surviving A Borderline Parent: How to Heal Your Childhood Wounds and Build Trust, Boundaries, and Self-Esteem.* Oakland, CA: New Harbinger Publications.

17. Rutledge, R. B., Skandali, N., Dayan, P., & Dolan, R. J. (2014). A computational and neural model of momentary subjective well-being. *Proceedings of the National Academy of Sciences,* 111 (33), 12252-12257.

18. Sherman, J. (2014, August 27). The secret to happiness and compassion: Low expectations. Psychology Today, https://www.psychologytoday.com/blog/ambigamy/201408/the-secret-happiness-and-compassion-low-expectations-expectations

19. Sinek, S. (September 29, 2013). "Start with Why." https://www.youtube.com/watch?v=sioZd3AxmnE

20. Thomas, M. L., Kaufmann, C. N., Palmer, B.W., et al. (2016). Paradoxical trend for improvement in mental health with aging: A community-based study of 1,456 adults aged 21-100 years. *Journal of Clinical Psychiatry,* 77 (8), e1019-e1025.

21. Vaillant, G. (2011). Involuntary coping mechanisms: A psychodynamic perspective. *Dialogues in Clinical Neuroscience,* 13(3), 366-370.

22. Williams, M. (2014). *Surviving the Toxic Family: Taking yourself out of the equation and taking your life back from your dysfunctional family.* MarinaWilliamsLMHC.com.

23. Wotitz, J. G. (1983). *Adult Children of Alcoholics.* Pompano Beach, FL: Health Communications, Inc.

24. Yudofsky, S. C. (2005). *Fatal flaws: Navigating Destructive Relationships With People With Disorders of Personality and Character.* Washington, DC: American Psychiatric Publishing.

ACKNOWLEGEMENTS

I am grateful to the many people whose encouragement gave me the audacity and stamina to complete this volume. These include my coaches, Robin Roberson and especially Mike Mirau of Proactive Leadership Group; my leading synergy partner for over twenty-five years, Chris Clausen of CNC Homecare; my psychology colleagues Dr. Don Weaver and Dr. Kevin Karlson; colleagues from the Dallas Executives Association, especially Dr. Maude Cejudo; my invaluable "in-house" business consultation and mentoring team, which includes my son, Simon Chafetz, and my stepsons, Andy Goldstein and David Goldstein; and my IT and marketing associate and good friend, Bill Greenberg.

I also deeply appreciate the friends and colleagues who read preliminary versions and provided valuable feedback, especially Doris Booth, Pam Boyd, Bruce Brafman, Howard Denemark, Ken Durand, Kay Hale, Liz Liener, Lisa Mach, Victor Molinari, Rona Train, Michael Wald, Myron Weiner, and Cedric Wood. My wonderful editor, Jon VanZile of Editing for Authors, improved my rough manuscript immensely.

I owe a special debt to my wife, Suzanne, who graciously allowed me to steal from our together time to complete this work.

Most of all, I am deeply indebted to my patients over the past thirty-five years, and their families, for allowing me to become privy to their innermost secrets. Ninety-nine percent of the material included in these pages, I learned through them. I hope that I have proven worthy of their confidence.

ABOUT THE AUTHOR

Dr. Paul Chafetz, clinical psychologist and former university associate professor, is a full-time private practitioner in Dallas, Texas. A native of Memphis, Tennessee, he earned his BA in psychology at Brown University and his PhD in clinical and health psychology at the University of Florida. He completed his pre-doctoral internship in clinical and health psychology at Duke University Medical Center and his post-doctoral fellowship in clinical gero-psychology at the Texas Research Institute for Mental Sciences in Houston.

He was a faculty member at The University of Texas Southwestern Medical Center in Dallas for nineteen years, teaching graduate courses in the psychology of aging. He has twice served as president of the Dallas Psychological Association. Learn more about him at PaulKChafetz.com.

NOTES

NOTES

NOTES

NOTES